With Child offers us a precious opportunity to read the B̶i̶b̶l̶e̶ through a mother's eyes. Danielle Jones writes as a mother about mothers, bringing Scripture to life in fresh and vivid ways. Without motherhood, we would have no God with us in the flesh. That alone is reason to pick up this book. Jones's beautiful storytelling and wise reflections give us many more.
—CHRISTIE PURIFOY, author of *Seedtime & Harvest*

With Child is a profoundly thought-provoking book. Despite my 25 years of biblical teaching, Danielle offers unique perspectives on women's lives in the Bible I had never previously thought. Her intentional style provides fresh insights into God's plan and instills renewed hope, reminding us that God remains close regardless of our paths.
—ALEX PENDUCK, Pastor & Author

Being a mother is lonely at times. It can feel like no one else understands our fears, longings, and heartaches. But in *With Child,* Danielle Ayers Jones beautifully reminds all of us called "mom" that we are not alone. She draws us into familiar narratives of women in Scripture and gives us fresh eyes to see them as flesh-and-blood women who do understand those fears, longings, and heartaches. And, as she does, she breathes fresh hope and camaraderie into the complex parts of your story and mine.
—ASHLEIGH SLATER, editor, co-host of the *Team Us* podcast

Danielle lays out beautiful examples of the power and purpose of mothering through the moms of the Bible. This book is an encouragement for moms in all seasons of life.
—BRENDA L. YODER, author of *Uncomplicated: Simple Secrets for a Compelling Life*

with child

In Christian art, the square halo identified a living person presumed to be a saint. Square Halo Books is devoted to publishing works that present contextually sensitive biblical studies and practical instruction consistent with the Doctrines of the Reformation. The goal of Square Halo Books is to provide materials useful for encouraging and equipping the saints.

©2024 Square Halo Books, Inc.
P.O. Box 18954
Baltimore, MD 21206
www.SquareHaloBooks.com

Scripture quotations are from The Holy Bible, English Standard Version® (ESV ®), copyright ©2001 by Crossway, a publishing ministry of Good News Publishers. Used by permission. All rights reserved.

ISBN 978-1-941106-39-6
Library of Congress Control Number: 2024944374

Printed in the United States of America

with child

ENCOUNTERING GOD ALONGSIDE
MOTHERS IN THE BIBLE

DANIELLE AYERS JONES

**SQUARE HALO
BOOKS**

This book is for Josh,
who encouraged me
from the beginning to end.

And for Owen, Duncan,
Sophia, and Ava.
You are my favorite
and my best.

Table of Contents

Introduction

NOTHING IS BEING WASTED

The technician ran the wand over my ever-enlarging belly at my first ultrasound. My husband, Josh, sat beside me at the end of the narrow bed. After only a few moments, the technician quickly pulled the wand off of my abdomen and looked at the screen again before turning towards me.

"Well," she said. "It looks like you're going to have twins!"

I stared back at her in utter shock. Then I started laughing rather hysterically.

I couldn't wrap my mind around the thought. I had just gotten used to the idea of being pregnant and ushering *one* child into the world. Now I was going to have two—at the same time!

I couldn't even imagine what life with twin babies would look like.

Thankfully, there were multiple women at my church who had twins and even my husband's aunt had a pair of fraternal twins—a boy and a girl. One of my co-workers was also pregnant with twins at the same that I was. People at church and work joked that there must be *something in the water.*

But when I told my grandmother, she didn't seem surprised.

"They run in the family," she explained. This was news to me. I didn't know a single family member with twins.

"My aunt had twins," she continued. "And we told all your

aunts they might have twins." That seemed to be as far as family knowledge went. My generation didn't know twins were a thing in our family, but that year, 2007, it was made clear that they did indeed run in the family, because my cousin became pregnant with fraternal twins as well.

My pregnancy progressed uneventfully. I traded in my *What to Expect When You're Expecting* for all the books about expecting multiples. I kept working until the doctor asked me to stop, which ended up being just five days before the twins arrived. They were born without a single complication—no need for a cesarean or the NICU.

One of my first comments upon finding out about this double blessing was, "How am I going to go to the grocery store?" We laughed about it later, because it seemed kind of silly, but for some reason the picture of a one-seated grocery cart loomed in my mind as an impossible challenge. Going to the grocery store didn't turn out to be a challenge after all: my husband took over that job, so it ended up being a long time until I could do the weekly grocery shopping again anyway. Though I knew other twin moms, I couldn't really anticipate how much my life would change when I had not just one baby, but two. I couldn't really picture what it would look like, however much I tried to plan for it.

At their two-week checkup the boys got a "failure to thrive" diagnosis, which brought about individual feedings every two hours, plus supplementing with formula by a bottle after each nursing. Each sleepy baby took about forty-five minutes to breastfeed, and it felt like half the time I was trying to keep them awake long enough to take in some nourishment. I had about a thirty-minute break before starting the whole process over again.

Time came to a standstill. As a new mom I had no idea how long this schedule would last but it seemed interminable. The ironic thing was that while I was physically working so hard, I was mentally bored out of my mind. I think this might have been the first time in my life I was actually bored, because being the creative person that I am, I usually always had an ongoing project to accomplish. But now I was home alone with infants all day every day. There was no need for anyone to help me—there was nothing they could really do anyway. There were no other children messing up the house or needing tending; it was just me needing to feed those baby boys for what felt like endless hours. Looking back, I realize I was probably mildly depressed.

Before birth, I had visions of nursing while quietly reading books multiple times a day like I'd seen my mother do. I had looked forward to this ideal. But nursing twins didn't allow for that ideal to come true—the reality was completely different from what I'd imagined. This was right before smartphones became ubiquitous, so there wa-s no Audible, no podcasts that I could easily access hands-free. I concocted a way to listen to audiobooks through our DVD player and listened to *Under the Tuscan Sun* while using the remote controls of the DVD player to turn it off and on from the couch in my living room.

I found myself daydreaming about my pre-baby life. The mundane life of commuting, work, and community now felt like a paradise. I'd left an exciting job in museum exhibitions, where I had spent my days invested in stimulating projects involving art and history, discussions with intelligent people, and lunches at local Indian or Japanese restaurants. Back when I was pregnant, I had thought I was ready for motherhood, but now, the reality of around-the-clock feedings left me feeling regret. What had I done? I'd traded in a job I loved and thrived at for fumbling through sleepless nights and mind-numbingly staring at a wall while nursing.

The transition hit me harder than I'd expected.

Then God sent me an insightful woman who was my first lactation consultant. She sized me up in a few swift minutes.

"You're a Type A person, aren't you?" she asked perceptively. I nodded. "What you need is to make nursing your boys your new job," she suggested. "You need to feel like you're accomplishing something. Make a spreadsheet and keep track of each feeding, check it off, whatever you need to do to see the progress you're making. We will track their weight weekly when you come in to weigh them."

When she made this observation about me, I almost wept. She recognized something of the inner struggle going on within me, and she offered me hope. For me, hope has never looked like wanting someone to sympathize with my emotions. Hope, for me, is a solution. She offered me something I could *do*. A way to feel productive again.

The truth was I felt guilty. I felt guilty about desperately wishing I could go back to my old life. Back to "before the boys." It wasn't that I didn't love my sons—although maybe I'd not completely bonded yet. It was simply that the task-oriented personality God put inside of me longed for more "productive" things to do besides feeding my boys every few hours. My Type A personality could barely stand all the time I was "wasting" by sitting around all day on the couch nursing.

Growing up I wanted to live a radical life for God. I imagined myself a modern Amy Carmichael living in a foreign country, doing mission work, and writing books. I devoured Elisabeth Elliot's narratives about missionary life in the jungle. Maybe I could write for a non-profit and spread their mission far and wide. I'd write the Great American Novel. I'd become a children's book illustrator like Tasha Tudor.

No ordinary life for me!

Yet here I was, staring at my walls, nursing my babies non-stop for the unforeseeable future. *How long was this going to last?* I wondered. The years seemed to stretch out before me. I felt like my life was at a standstill, every day so very much the same. I'd been looking forward to my schedule slowing down, but I wasn't prepared for how slowly the hours in the house would crawl by some days, despite the fact that I barely had time to do anything other than change diapers and feed the babies!

My life had become quite ordinary. Instead of the radical life I'd envisioned, I was a stay-at-home mom doing—what I perceived to be—absolutely nothing. And producing milk was *not* the type of productivity I'd envisioned.

But it was in the very mundane task of making sure infant babies were fed that I encountered God in a very real way.

One day God clearly spoke to my heart and in one moment, he impressed on me this very important truth that cut to the core of my discontentment:

Nothing is being wasted.

This was the message that rang clear in my head. This is the whisper spoken directly to my heart. It is like someone spoke the words out loud: *nothing is being wasted*. I am spending my time growing and nurturing two little babies that God created, and this is good and important work. This realization hit me hard and transformed my attitude, mindset, and outlook. Most of all, it gave me comfort.

I was reminded of Colossians 3:23, which says, "Whatever you do, do it from the heart, as something done for the Lord and not for people" (CSB). Instead of mindless drudgery, I recognized that I could offer my work as an act of worship to the Lord. I knew this intellectually all along, but its application to my life in this area was fresh. It had been easier to apply when I was working a job I loved. Now it was hard. It was no longer just something I mentally agreed to but now it was something I would have to live out in a new, unseen way. When the Holy Spirit whispered those words into my heart, it was a God encounter that reshaped my motherhood from that point forward.

Eventually, I began looking forward to spending my time feeding the boys as a time of bonding with them. They successfully gained weight. They became more alert. They started to develop personalities. They learned what they were doing. I learned what I was doing. Feeding time evolved into a time to connect with God. I used the time of forced stillness to pray for my new sons as well as my family and friends. What I couldn't know then was that this specific time of forced slow living would actually be a very short period of my life. Then came the day Josh's aunt walked in with dinner and her twin nursing pillow. She taught me how to successfully tandem nurse and it felt like the gates of heaven opened and I finally could start doing other things besides sitting on the couch again. There even came a point when I could read while nursing!

However, this lesson of *nothing is wasted* would be one I'd encounter again and again in different ways over the years. I was just at the very beginning of discovering God in this journey called motherhood. It was the beginning of seeing how motherhood could be the conduit for encountering God in a whole new way. Nothing makes us quite so desperate as motherhood. Desperate for sleep, desperate for the safety of our children, desperate—ultimately—for God himself. For his strength, his wisdom, and his comfort.

It turns out to be a pretty radical way to live after all.

HOW MOTHERHOOD REFLECTS GOD

Perhaps one reason motherhood has the possibility to connect us more closely to God is that motherhood itself reflects something of God's character and personhood. Genesis 1:27 reminds us, "So God created man in his own image, in the image of God he created him; male and female he created them." Being female is a connection to one aspect of God. Both men and women are formed in his image; part of God's identity exists within both sexes.

Beyond that, God specifically associated himself with the trials of motherhood in his relationship with Israel on multiple occasions. With the language of childbearing, he lamented his children's rebellious ways and reminded them of who he was in Isaiah 46:3–4:

Listen to me, house of Jacob,
all the remnant of the house of Israel,

who have been sustained from the womb,
carried along since birth.
I will be the same until your old age,
and I will bear you up when you turn gray.
I have made you, and I will carry you;
I will bear and rescue you. (CSB)

Here God is like a mother, carrying Israel like a baby
wrapped in a carrier. His care is personal and tender; he never
gives up on us, even when we are old and gray.

God also used the language of motherhood when he
reminded Israel that he would never forget them in Isaiah 49:15:

Can a mother forget the baby at her breast
and have no compassion on the child she has borne?
Though she may forget,
I will not forget you! (NIV)

God represents the perfect mother in this passage, never
abandoning his children, never forgetting them, but instead
always remembering them.

And in a hymn of praise, God rejoiced over Israel comparing
himself to a mother comforting a child in Isaiah 66:7–13:

Before Zion was in labor, she gave birth;
before she was in pain, she delivered a boy.
Who has heard of such a thing?
Who has seen such things?
Can a land be born in one day
or a nation be delivered in an instant?

Yet as soon as Zion was in labor,
she gave birth to her sons.
"Will I bring a baby to the point of birth
and not deliver it?"
says the LORD;
"or will I who deliver, close the womb?"
says your God.
Be glad for Jerusalem and rejoice over her,
all who love her.
Rejoice greatly with her,
all who mourn over her—
so that you may nurse and be satisfied
from her comforting breast
and drink deeply and delight yourselves
from her glorious breasts.

For this is what the LORD says:

I will make peace flow to her like a river,
and the wealth of nations like a flood;
you will nurse and be carried on her hip
and bounced on her lap.
As a mother comforts her son,
so I will comfort you,
and you will be comforted in Jerusalem. (CSB)

God aligned himself with motherhood in the most intimate
way possible. God was the "perfect parent." He did everything
right. There was nothing for him to feel guilty about. There
was nothing he could wish to go back and do differently.

He regretted none of his parenting choices. Yet despite his perfection, he knew the sting of watching his children suffer, the hurt of watching his children abandon him for false gods, as Israel repeatedly did. And not only does God reflect aspects of motherhood himself, but he is also very concerned with the lives of mothers, as shown in so many stories in the Bible. Whether we see him strengthening Hagar when she essentially became a single mother, answering Hannah's prayer for a child, or providing for the practical needs of the widow of Zarephath, God shows us that he is willing to encounter us in our need.

And so, we can bring all our joys, triumphs, fears, and griefs to him. He knows all about them. *Nothing is being wasted when it comes to God.* No matter what kind of mother we've been, or are, or will be, he'll never leave, because after all, we're his children too.

Stories of mothers are sown throughout Scripture, and it has been my joy to study these stories, looking to discover how these women encountered God. This book is meant to be read with your Bible open beside you, as we'll experience these stories from Scripture together and spend time reflecting upon and responding in prayer to them. You can use this book individually (perhaps with a journal to record your thoughts) or with a group, using the "Getting to the Heart" section to help discuss each woman's story and discover how her God encounter can impact our own lives. It is my hope that whether you read this book alone or with a group, these biblical women will guide you to have your own God encountering moment. I don't know what you need, but God does. May God use this book to provide comfort, strength, encouragement, and hope for whatever situation you are facing in your own story.

Eve

THE FIRST LIFE GIVER

The ground is hard beneath her hips. Sweat slides down her back and every muscle strains. Eve closes her eyes tight as another contraction twists deep in her abdomen, feeling like it will tear her apart.

Her mind recalls the Creator's words after she ate the forbidden fruit: "I will intensify your labor pains; you will bear children with painful effort" (Gen. 3:16 CSB). Was the pain wracking her body right now what he meant?

The discomfort is almost unbearable. Fear grips her. She gives a powerful push as another contraction washes over her.

After several more excruciating, burning pushes, a head emerges. Just when she feels like she can't stand it anymore, shoulders push through next. Then she hears a cry.

The first new life is born into the world: a son.

Eve leans back onto a heap of animal skins as her body relaxes for the first time in hours while Adam cleanses off the residue of birth with water from a hollowed out wooden basin. Wrapping the infant in a skin, he hands the child to Eve.

"I have had a baby boy with the Lord's help," breathes Eve, looking into her son's dark and squinting eyes for the first time. "Let's call him Cain," Eve says, looking up at Adam, who smiles.

THE FIRST NEW MOTHER

I can't imagine the fear that must have gripped Eve during her first birth. There was no copy of *What to Expect When You're Expecting* available to be purchased at the local bookstore. She had no mother to describe birth or give her an encouraging pep talk. No nurses or midwives stood beside her, reminding her to breathe. Only Adam was there—as clueless as she was. How did they know to cut the umbilical cord or to get the baby to nurse?

Each milestone of their baby's new life was new to them, as no one had ever seen a human grow from baby to adulthood before.

No doubt baby Cain brought a newfound joy into Adam and Eve's lives. And later another son, Abel, was added to their family.

But bliss was not to be had outside of Eden.

Sin—and ultimately death itself—had entered the world when Adam and Eve disregard God's instructions and instead listened to the serpent who tempted them to bite into the luscious-looking fruit from the tree of the knowledge of good and evil. This became apparent all too soon, when Adam and Eve suddenly felt the shame of their nakedness, something they'd never experienced before. Hiding their bodies behind fig leaves, they also tried to hide their now sinful selves from God's presence but found they could not. Their actions ushered in death, both physically and spiritually. No longer could they walk with God in the garden of Eden in the cool of the day. Instead, they were driven from that place of spiritual communion and easy stewardship to sweat and labor in order to keep themselves alive. Adam and Eve would also come to realize and experience the human capacity for evil to lodge itself in their hearts—to the point that one human would choose to actually *force* death on another against their will.

At the hands of his jealous brother, Abel crumpled to a heap in the fields in what was the first recorded death in Scripture. As far as we know, the first death outside of Eden was not a natural one—it was also the first murder. Eve's heart was the first mother's heart to ache at the loss of her child at the hands of violence. The perpetrator was not an unknown assailant, but her own firstborn son, Cain. How her heart must have broken—twice.

It might have been easy for Eve to blame herself for one son's crime and the other's death: *If only I hadn't listened to the serpent. If only I'd not eaten the fruit.* Or perhaps she may have laid the blame elsewhere: *If only Adam had stopped me and not tasted it with me. If only God had given us another chance and not thrown us out of Eden.*

We do not know if Eve was tempted to think in this way. But in our last glimpse of her in the Genesis account, we see trust and hope: "And Adam knew his wife again, and she bore a son and called his name Seth, for she said, 'God has appointed for me another offspring instead of Abel, for Cain killed him.' To Seth also a son was born, and he called his name Enosh. At that time people began to call upon the name of the Lord" (Gen. 4:25–26). In these final recorded words of Eve, she demonstrated trust in God's provision. He granted her another son, Seth, and with Seth's birth came the hope of a new beginning, new life. And during Seth's lifetime, people began to call upon the name of the Lord—they turned from the heritage of death Cain brought into the world towards the hope of life that Seth brought with him.

Eve's Legacy

This hope of new life leads us to the very meaning of Eve's name. Even though it was through Adam and Eve's eating of the forbidden fruit that sin and death corrupted the world, sin and death are not Eve's ultimate legacy.

We do not learn Eve's name until *after* the fall into sin. First, the woman received the consequences of listening to the serpent's lies from God himself: "I will intensify your labor pains; you will bear children with painful effort. Your desire will be for your husband, yet he will rule over you" (Gen. 3:16 CSB). Then Adam received his: "You will eat bread by the sweat of your brow until you return to the ground, since you were taken from it. For you are dust, and you will return to dust" (Gen. 3:19 CSB). It's right after God's pronouncement of death that we see a glimmer of hope, life, and salvation. It was after Eve tasted the fruit—which ushered in death—that she was given her name: "The man called his wife's name Eve, because she was the mother of all living. And the Lord God made for Adam and for his wife garments of skins and clothed them" (Gen. 3:20–21).

Right there, sandwiched between the consequences of sin and the first animal sacrifice also due to that sin, we have Eve's true legacy: *life.* Her name comes from the Hebrew meaning "life-giver" "to give life" or "to breathe." She was the mother of all living and breathing humans, and this very fact gives humanity its future hope. And in that first animal sacrifice we see God tenderly clothe Adam and Eve, replacing their crude attempts at flimsy, fig-leaf clothing with a more durable and lasting covering for their shame.

Eventually, Eve's own offspring would give the serpent his deathblow. Eve must have held that hope close to her heart, although she could not understand its full future ramifications. For in God's curse to the serpent, he made it clear that the serpent wouldn't succeed in his plan: "I will put enmity between you and the woman, and between your offspring and her offspring; he shall bruise your head, and you shall bruise his heel" (Gen. 3:15). Later in the Bible, the serpent's fate is more clearly revealed in Revelation 12:9 where it says, "So the great dragon was thrown out—*the ancient serpent*, who is called the devil and Satan, the one who deceives the whole world. He was thrown to earth, and his angels with him" (CSB, emphasis mine). Eve's God encounter might at first only sound like curses, but God intended to use her to reverse the curse in the end. Paul explained it this way, "Therefore, just as sin came into the world through one man [Adam], and death through sin, and so death spread to all men because all sinned . . . For as by the one man's disobedience the many were made sinners, so by the one man's [Jesus'] obedience the many will be made righteous." (Rom. 5:12, 19). Although Eve ushered in sin and death through her own actions and her influence over Adam to sin with her, her family line would produce a future Savior, Jesus, and she would have a part to play in that redemption story.

Eve was the first life-giver from whose line would come the ultimate life-giver: Jesus. The one who reversed the curse of death, once and for all.

EVE'S GOD ENCOUNTER

Even though Eve's actions brought sin and death into the world, her legacy is one of hope and promise. It can be found in her very name, Eve, which means *life*. As the story of redemption began to unfold, God had a plan to use Eve in that redemption process.

GETTING TO THE HEART

Read Genesis 1–4.

Think of a time when you failed or sinned to an extent that you felt there was no hope for you.

How does Eve's legacy of life—despite her sin—offer you a personal glimpse of hope and redemption for your situation?

How can Eve's life show you that there's always hope after sin and that no sin is too big for God to redeem?

A Prayer for Fresh Hope

LORD, LIKE EVE I'VE FAILED.
Sometimes it feels like I can't get past
my failures. Please help me remember not to put
my faith in myself. My faith is in you. You have
made me and redeemed me. I cannot escape your
love, forgiveness, and faithfulness. You work through
my failures and offer me not perfection, but your
own perfect self. You offer redemption for all my
past failures and sins. Thank you that even though
I can't live a perfect life, you lived, died,
and rose to life in my place.

Sarah

A WOMAN OF PARADOX

Sarah sits at the tent door, listening to the conversation outside, which is turning out to be quite extraordinary. Earlier that day, three strange men had appeared and put Abraham in a tizzy. He burst into the tent and told Sarah to quickly make cakes of bread. He rushed out to the herd of cattle and selected a calf and butchered it. He prepared a meal for the men—curds, milk, meat, and bread—and they'd all gathered together under the oak trees to eat.

Suddenly, one of the strange men speaks her name.

"About this time next year, Sarah will have a son," the man says.

Sarah laughs quietly to herself at this pronouncement. She can't help it; she is ninety years old. All these years she's longed for a child and now these strangers show up with this ridiculous prophecy! Although Abraham told her the Lord had promised him an heir, she had given up hoping. Her childbearing days were long over. It would take a miracle now.

The man's next words silence her laughter. "Why did Sarah laugh and say, 'Shall I indeed bear a child, now that I am old?'" the man asks. "Is anything too hard for the Lord? At the appointed time I will return to you, about this time next year, and Sarah will have a son."

Sarah is shocked that he seems to see into her mind. Who

is this man, this stranger, this visitor, who can read her deepest thoughts? Afraid and feeling a bit foolish, Sarah sheepishly comes out of the tent.

"I did not laugh," she says.

The man looks at her, "No, but you did laugh."

Sarah says nothing else. There isn't anything else to say.

A Defining Shame

"Hi, my name is Sarah and I'm barren."

Much like an alcoholic attending her first AA meeting, Sarah wore her barrenness as a defining shame, like a sin that someone needed to confess.

It's hard for us—living in the twenty-first century—to understand the shame that would have accompanied barrenness. We understand, perhaps, the disappointment. We imagine—or have even experienced—the sadness of not having a biological child when we'd hoped and planned for one. But it's hard to comprehend how, for a woman in Sarah's ancient time and culture, producing children—and more importantly a *son*—defined a woman's life and worth. To not have the prestige of bearing children would have been more than devastating. Later, women like Rachel and Elizabeth would connect their barrenness with being a "reproach," "humiliation," or "disgrace" (Gen. 30:23, Luke 1:25).

Sarah left her family and her home city of Ur to follow Abraham when he was called to journey to the land of Canaan. God promised to make Abraham a great nation. We learn that Sarah was so beautiful that at one point while traveling Abraham feared that the leaders of other nations would desire her and put his life in danger. To protect himself, he pretended she was his sister instead, giving her to Pharaoh when they visited Egypt due to famine. Thankfully, God intervened and despite Abraham's cowardly behavior, the two were reunited once Pharaoh discovered the truth (Gen. 12:10–20). But it was not until Sarah started to struggle with the reality of her barrenness that the real woman began to emerge, someone impatient with God's timing and lacking trust in his plan, someone who took matters into her own hands.

Someone I can identify with.

Eventually, Sarah decided enough was enough: she would have a child through Hagar, her Egyptian maidservant. She had given God time to act. Ten years, in fact, she'd waited for him to follow through on his initial promise (Gen. 16:3). She presented Abraham with the idea of marrying Hagar so that, essentially, Hagar would become a surrogate mother for Sarah. Hagar was a slave, so her thoughts or feelings on the subject were of no account to Sarah. However, God had already spoken to Abraham and made a covenant with him. God had clearly told him that "your very own son shall be your heir" (Gen. 15:4). Not only that, but his offspring would eventually number as vast as the stars in heaven. And Abraham believed God. But maybe, he too began to doubt God's promise. Maybe, since Sarah was not specifically named as the mother of that heir, both Sarah and Abraham began to think God would provide a son through someone other than Sarah. Sarah was not named in the covenant promise until after the Hagar debacle. In Genesis 17:16 God made it *very* clear, saying, "I will bless her, and moreover, I will give you a son by her. I will bless her, and she shall become nations; kings of peoples shall come from her." Was the fact that Sarah was not explicitly named earlier the reason Sarah felt like she'd found a loophole? We don't know. What we do know is Abraham listened to Sarah's unwise plan to finally get the child they longed for, by using her maidservant as a surrogate.

Hagar conceived. We don't know what she thought about her change of status within the household. Perhaps she resented being forced to marry Abraham? Or perhaps she was proud of her move up to the status of wife within the household? It seems like the latter was probably her perspective because now that Hagar had what Sarah so desperately wanted, she viewed Sarah with disdain and scorn (Gen. 16:4).

Things got tense—and as dramatic as a soap opera—in Abraham's tent. Instead of repenting for her actions, Sarah began to blame the whole thing on Abraham as if it had all been his idea. She took out her frustration and anger on a pregnant Hagar, and here we see Sarah at her worst. She became vindictive and abusive.

So Hagar fled. (We'll come back to Hagar later. She deserves a chapter of her own.)

Sarah's mistreatment of Hagar made everyone's life miserable, to the point that Hagar was willing to risk being alone in the wilderness rather than continue to live with Abraham and Sarah. It must have gotten pretty bad. But there was still hope for Sarah, just as there is hope for us.

In the end, Hagar came back, and life went on as normally as possible for a while.

Then the three mysterious visitors arrive and upend Sarah's world with their announcement. Sarah's long wait is finally over. By the following year Sarah will have her longed-for baby.

Sarah laughs in disbelief, but then, immediately denies it out of fear. This seems to be the first time Sarah has experienced a personal encounter with God, so a bit of holy trembling is to be expected. Thus far, Abraham has been the only one to receive messages from the Lord. No doubt he shares these experiences with Sarah, but not having had personal communication with God may have contributed to Sarah's lack of belief up to this point.

This time, the promise is not relayed secondhand. Sarah meets these holy visitors for herself and is *personally* promised her son.

A PROMISE COMES TRUE

God's promise to Sarah becomes a flesh and blood son she can hold in her wrinkled arms. Her joy overflows when she exclaims, "God has made laughter for me; everyone who hears will laugh over me.... Who would have said to Abraham that Sarah would nurse children? Yet I have borne him a son in his old age" (Gen. 21:6-7). Despite Sarah's impatience and her attempts to take control, God still comes through on his promise in his own time.

Looking back at these episodes in Sarah's life, it would be easy to focus only on her impatience and abusive treatment of Hagar. God does not sweep this failing under the rug—it's there for all of us to see. Yet amazingly, this is not her legacy. It is not how she's remembered. Her failures are there for us to relate to and learn from. As a twenty-first century woman I might not be able to relate to asking my husband to marry a slave and have a child for me, but in what other ways do I act in unbelief

towards God's promises and strike out on my own? Do I ever
try to manipulate people or circumstances to get my way? Do
I ever blame others for my own failures of judgment instead
of repenting and taking responsibility for my own actions? No
doubt there are times that I do.

A WOMAN OF FAITH

Even with all these examples of unbelief, Sarah was the
first woman recorded in the list of people who lived by faith in
Hebrews: "By *faith* Sarah herself received power to conceive,
even when she was past the age, since she considered him
faithful who had promised" (Heb. 11:11, emphasis mine). Could
this be the same woman we see in Genesis?

Yes, it is. Because laughing in the tent wasn't the end of
Sarah's story. In the end she laughed for joy. She laughed
because the whole thing was something only God could do.
Sarah put her faith in God, regardless of her previous failures.
Sarah left her homeland, her family, and a life of comfort to
follow Abraham into a life of wandering because God asked
him to do so. She gave all of that up so that Abraham could
follow God's call. And at long last, when she was physically past
getting pregnant, she finally had her own experience with God
and was given her long-promised son when only God could
have made it happen.

The woman who once struggled with unbelief is now known
for her faith. What a paradox! But isn't that like God? He takes
our biggest struggle and works something good out of it. Even if
my faith is faltering today, there is hope for a faith-filled future.

By faith, I too can have an assurance and a conviction that God is working his plan out in my life, even if in the past I've acted out in disbelief.

Despite my past, just like Sarah, I too can leave a legacy of faith.

Sarah's God Encounter:

Sarah shows us the importance of waiting for God's perfect timing and not manipulating circumstances to our own benefit. Even though Sarah was impatient and unbelieving, God's redemption is evident, as Sarah is the first of only two women mentioned by name in the list of those who live by faith in Hebrews 11. Although we see Sarah's failures, she is not defined by them—God's faithfulness shines through.

GETTING TO THE HEART

Read Genesis 16–18:15; 21:1–7; Hebrews 11:11.

In what area have you had to put aside your own timing for something and instead wait for God's?

Have you blamed someone else for decisions or failures that are entirely your own? If so, how can you make that right before God and the person that you blamed?

How has God shown his faithfulness to you in the past, and how can this build your faith for the future?

A Prayer for Faith

LORD, SO OFTEN MY FAITH IS SHAKY,
misplaced, or nonexistent. Like Sarah I try
to take matters into my own hands. I manipulate
the situation instead of trusting you when I know
I should. I long for things—good things—you've
not yet granted me. I become jealous when other
people get what I want. Forgive me. Help me grow to
trust you more. Even if my faith is small like a mustard
seed, may it take root and grow stronger every day.

Hagar

TRUST IN THE WILDERNESS

Hagar collapses at a spring in the middle of the wilderness. Cupping dusty hands, she lifts cool water to her mouth and wipes her sweltering face with relief.

She is running from the cruel treatment of her mistress Sarah, Abraham's wife. How desperate she must have been to run into the wilderness, pregnant. But the Lord sees Hagar's plight as she tries to regain her strength at the spring. It is not yet time for her to leave Abraham's household.

"Hagar, servant of Sarah, where have you come from and where are you going?" An angel appears before her and questions her. Does she think she is seeing a mirage?

"I am fleeing from my mistress," Hagar freely admits.

"Return to your mistress and submit to her," the angel tells her. "I will multiply your offspring so that they cannot be numbered." Then, the angel goes on to promise Hagar a son who will go by the name of Ishmael, because the Lord had seen and listened to Hagar's suffering.

This news means an attitude adjustment on Hagar's part. No more lording it over Sarah's head that she is with child and Sarah is not. But there are no guarantees that Sarah will suddenly treat her with kindness. The angel of the Lord simply asks her to obey his words.

Still, she is given a promise to hold onto. She will bear a son she will name him Ishmael, meaning, "God hears." With this assurance, Hagar's heart lifts to praise: "You are a God of seeing," she says of the Lord, giving him the name El Roi. "Truly here I have seen him who looks after me" (Gen. 16:13). Hagar—Egyptian, servant, outsider—has a God encounter that is possibly the most intimate and direct for a woman in the Bible since Eve's story.

Hagar, in contrast to Sarah, is a wonderful example of trusting God in a hard family dynamic. Being Egyptian, it would be likely that Hagar worshiped pagan Egyptian gods before this experience in the wilderness. How had she viewed the God of Abraham and Sarah before this moment? Had Sarah's actions towards her discredited the God of Israel in Hagar's eyes? We don't know.

But a personal experience with God changed things for Hagar. In the wilderness she meets a God who sees her distress and personally responds to her situation, giving her hope. Her suffering does not go unnoticed.

Hagar trusts God with her very uncertain future. Although God gives her a promise, she doesn't know how things are going to turn out. With fewer promises than Sarah had, Hagar's faith is really quite amazing. Picking herself off the dusty ground, she puts trust into action and obeys God. Hagar goes back to serve Abraham and Sarah and gives birth to Ishmael.

THE GOD WHO SEES

Sixteen or seventeen years passed and Hagar once again found herself in the wilderness. This time she was being sent out of Abraham's house—for good. Although Sarah instigated Hagar's leaving, it was the Lord who ultimately confirmed to Abraham

that the time had come for Ishmael to leave. And again, the Lord
intervened in what looked like a desperate situation.

Running out of the bread and water Abraham provided her,
Hagar made her weak son comfortable under a bush, out from
under the hot sun, and awaited death. Tears ran down her dusty
face. She moved a little away from Ishmael so that she wouldn't
have to watch him die.

Did Hagar wonder about the promises she received from
God when she was pregnant with Ishmael? Did she think all
was lost? That God had forgotten her?

No, God had not forgotten her. God heard Hagar and
Ishmael's cries for help:

> God heard the boy crying, and the angel of God called
> to Hagar from heaven and said to her, "What's wrong,
> Hagar? Don't be afraid, for God has heard the boy crying
> from the place where he is. Get up, help the boy up, and
> grasp his hand, for I will make him a great nation." Then
> God opened her eyes, and she saw a well. So she went and
> filled the waterskin and gave the boy a drink. God was
> with the boy, and he grew; he settled in the wilderness and
> became an archer. He settled in the Wilderness of Paran,
> and his mother got a wife for him from the land of Egypt.
> (Genesis 21:17–21 CSB)

God once again responded to Hagar's need by providing life-
giving water. He also reiterated a promise to give her much-
needed hope for her future and that of her son. As Leigh McLeroy
put it in her book *Treasured: Knowing God by the Things He Keeps*:

All-seeing God also opened the eyes of desperate Hagar, and she saw a well of water that must have been there all along. Maybe she had even glanced at it before and simply moved on, assuming it was as dry and empty as she was. Redirected to the well, she filled the parched waterskin with fresh, soothing water and gave her son a drink. And she drank in the knowledge that the God she'd once named El Roi, or "the one who sees," had seen her in her first flight and was seeing her still.[1]

Hagar and Ishmael lived, making a home in the wilderness. Whether the water had been there all along and Hagar had missed it, or God miraculously provided it at that moment, we don't know. But once again, Hagar experienced God's personal care. She and her son were not forgotten.

Both times, it was in the wilderness that God met with Hagar and gave her the strength for what lay ahead. Isn't that the way God so often works?

That's how it's been in my life. In the darkest, most helpless moments, I experience God's presence and care in a way like never before. Even if I feel small, misused, ill-treated, and unloved, I have a God who sees. Even if I fear for my child's uncertain future, I have a God who sees. No matter what the diagnosis, I have a God who sees. No matter the prodigal child, I have a God who sees. No matter the financial distress, I have a God who sees. No matter the marital problem, I have a God who sees.

I want to respond to God like Hagar did. But so often I'm more like Sarah. I know God's promises by heart—have heard them for years—but so often I doubt. I decide to try it my own way. Instead, I want to trust like Hagar.

Even in the wilderness.

Hagar's God Encounter:

God's own people, Abraham and Sarah, treated Hagar wrongly. The Bible doesn't gloss over this fact. But during her most desperate moments in the wilderness, God meets with Hagar. Hagar shows us what it means to trust God, "the one who sees," even in the toughest of situations.

Getting to the Heart

Read Genesis 16; 21:1–21.

Do you sometimes feel misused? Or maybe just invisible, like no one cares about how you're doing or what you do?

How can knowing that God is El Roi, the God who sees, encourage you today?

Is there a situation in your life or the life of your child that you view as desperate? How can knowing that God sees you give you the strength to keep going?

A Prayer for Trust

LORD, THERE ARE SITUATIONS SO DESPERATE
there's no way I can seem to think or work or pray
my way out of them. I am completely helpless. I'm at
the mercy of a person or a circumstance where there
seems to be no relief. My child's situation is one that
I can't seem to parent her out of. I know you are El Roi,
the God who sees. You see my situation and you will
provide me with sustaining strength each day to meet
what the day brings. Grant me the trust of Hagar.

Rebekah

A LEGACY OF DIVISION

It is evening as Rebekah walks down the well-worn path to the city of Nahor's well to draw water as she usually does each day. She nudges her way between tired travelers and other young women who are there to draw water just like she is. She bends down to the spring, fills her water jar, and then begins walking back towards home.

Suddenly, a man she doesn't know runs up to her and asks, "Please, may I have a little water to drink from your jar?"

"Drink, my lord," she replies. She hands him her jar and watches as he thirstily drinks the cool liquid. She notices his camels tied up not far behind him and realizes he has no way to water them.

"I will draw water for your camels too, if you wish," she says.

"Thank you," the man accepts her offer. She empties the rest of the water from her jar into the animal trough and runs back to the well to draw more water so the animals will have enough to quench their thirst.

The man sits in silence while she does all of this. Then, when her work is done, he does something that surprises her.

He offers her a gold ring and two bracelets, saying, "Please tell me whose daughter you are and if there is room in your father's house to spend the night?"

"I am the daughter of Bethuel and we have plenty of straw for your camels and room for you to spend the night," she says, slipping the bracelets on her arm.

The man follows her home. Once his camels are bedded down for the night, he reveals his true mission: to find a wife for his master's son. The servant shares that he asked God for a sign to determine the woman who would be the right bride for Isaac, his master Abraham's son. He tells Rebekah's father and brother that the sign he asked for was that the girl who offered to draw water for his camels would be the woman the Lord had chosen. Rebekah's father and brother agree that it seems to be God's providential will for Rebekah.

The next morning Abraham's servant makes preparations to leave. Her family requests that she spend ten more days with them before leaving. The servant refuses, however, saying they must leave immediately. Rebekah's opinion is sought: will she leave with this strange man and journey to meet a husband she's never met? Rebekah agrees to leave with the servant that day, and soon Rebekah and her nurse begin the journey to Canaan.

As they near her new home, Rebekah scans the horizon for a sign of her prospective husband and sees a figure in the distance walking in the field towards them. Getting off her camel, she questions the servant, "Who is that coming towards us?"

"He is my master," confirms the servant. Rebekah takes her veil and covers her face and stands quietly aside until the servant tells Isaac all that had happened on his trip. Then Isaac comes towards her with smiling eyes and an outstretched hand and takes Rebekah to be his wife and loves her.

FATEFUL FAVORITISM

For the next twenty years, Rebekah was barren, not unlike her mother-in-law Sarah. Twenty years in which Rebekah and Isaac had time to build a strong marriage. And they seemed to do so. Isaac loved his wife and prayed for her barrenness to be lifted. There was no mention of Isaac marrying other wives to try to have children through any other means but that which God had provided. And at long last Rebekah finally conceived—twins! However, her pregnancy was so tumultuous as the two children seemed to fight within her that she asked the Lord, "Why is this happening to me?"

The Lord directly answered her question, telling her two nations were in her womb and that the older one would ultimately serve the younger son.

Was it this prophecy of the older serving the younger that made Rebekah prefer Jacob to Esau? Did she tell Isaac or keep what the Lord said to her to herself? Or was it just that Rebekah and Jacob had similar interests and personalities, making their relationship easy?

Regardless, Scripture gives us a clue that a division is beginning to occur in Rebekah and Isaac's marriage, even after twenty years of being together: "Isaac loved Esau because he ate of his game, but Rebekah loved Jacob" (Gen. 25:28). A schism began to form in their family, with disastrous consequences.

Esau, the firstborn, was an outdoorsy man and a skillful hunter. Jacob was called "a quiet man" who stuck close to home (Gen. 25:27). Esau seemed to do whatever his emotions told him to, while Jacob quietly schemed, looking for an opportunity to exploit his brother. Esau—acting on impulse brought on by hunger and exhaustion—foolishly sold his birthright to Jacob. He didn't seem to think anything at all of selling his firstborn status to Jacob—he either disregarded its importance or didn't think doing so would have any lasting effect on his life. Or maybe he didn't really think it mattered since they were twins? Regardless, there was only one more thing Jacob needed to do to totally usurp his brother.

One day Rebekah overheard Isaac talking to Esau, the eldest of the twin boys. Discovering that her husband was planning on passing the blessing that God had given to Abraham onto Esau, she may have panicked. Hadn't God clearly promised before Jacob and Esau's birth that Esau would serve Jacob? What was happening? Something had to be done!

Rebekah wasted no time. Like Sarah before her, she came up with a plan to *make* God's will happen. She did not inquire of the Lord this time. She masterminded a plot to deceive her husband and cheat Esau so that Jacob could prosper. And in doing so, she ends up plunging her family into chaos.

Although Rebekah began her marriage full of trust in God, willing even to follow a stranger to another land to marry a man she did not know, she must have decided that God needed some help. She had no qualms about what she was doing. So much so that when Jacob brought up a concern with her plan, she boldly proclaimed, "Let your curse be on me, my son; only obey my voice, and go" (Gen. 27:13). She plotted for Jacob to impersonate Esau so that he would receive the eldest son's blessing, which Isaac was preparing to give Esau. Because Isaac's vision was impaired, she dressed Jacob in Esau's clothes and pretended that the delicious meal they'd prepared was game hunted by Esau instead of goats from their own flock. The plot worked. Isaac seemed a bit suspicious at first, but he believed Jacob—who insisted he was actually Esau. Isaac blessed Jacob with the firstborn's blessing that echoed the promise God made to Abraham—that one day their family would grow into a nation—and established Jacob's rule over his brother. But then Esau found out and flew into a murderous rage. Jacob had to go on the run to save his life.

Whatever Isaac and Rebekah's marriage had been in the beginning, no trust or respect seemed to be left. Their allegiances were to their children, not each other. Their children had driven them apart and now their family unit was divided into one that consisted of Rebekah and Jacob versus Isaac and Esau. They were not for each other, but instead each parent was actively working against one son and for the other. Isaac and Rebekah's family dynamics read as a cautionary tale.

As mothers we are busy raising our children. We care for their physical needs. We further their educational accomplishments. We help them cultivate athletic or artistic pursuits. We sacrifice for them in many ways. And all that may be good, *unless* we put our children before God or before our relationships with our spouses. Although we might not realize it, our children will suffer if we put them first to an unhealthy extent. And so will our marriages. No one purposefully wants to wake up when their kids are gone and realize they're now living with a stranger. And yet sometimes the choices we make *today* will create that future outcome if we allow our children to drive a wedge in our marriage like Rebekah and Isaac did.

Rebekah paid a heavy price for her deception in putting Jacob first. Despite her personal encounter with God in the past, she didn't seem to seek his wisdom when it came to raising her children after they were born. She relied on her own manipulation. When Jacob fled from Esau, who was now so angry that he was out to kill him, it was the last time she saw her favorite son as far as we know. Eventually, some twenty years later, Jacob was reunited with his father and was forgiven by Esau. But Rebekah did not live to see it.

Nor did she live to see that the hatred of Esau would last into future generations. Esau would father the Edomites, who would be Israel's enemy for many centuries.

Rebekah's legacy sobers me. It reminds me that my actions can tear down my own home: "Every wise woman builds her house, but a foolish one tears it down with her own hands" (Prov. 14:1 CSB). I may start out seeking God's will, but may end up trying to force my own will on my kids. Rebekah's story reminds me how much power I have over my children as well as my husband—for good or bad. We have to trust God for our children's futures, not manipulate their future like Rebekah did. However, if we have already messed up in the past or continue to make mistakes in the future, let's go to the one who's sovereign over all our futures. He will forgive us and help us begin again. Let's remember the young Rebekah who went to God with her questions and seek to foster family relationships of unity instead of division.

Rebekah's God Encounter:

The devastating effects of favoritism in marriage and family are played out in Isaac and Rebekah's story. Although Rebekah trusted in God's sovereignty early in her life, when it came to her children she no longer sought God or trusted in his leading but instead manipulated their future. By putting her children over her marriage, she destroyed the unity of her family.

GETTING TO THE HEART

Read Genesis 24–25; 27.

Is there some aspect of your life where you're investing in your children at the expense of your marriage? If so, where does change need to begin?

Favoritism is often not purposeful. It may be very subtle. Are there any aspects of favoritism between certain children that need to be considered?

Is there any *perceived* favoritism that needs to be addressed?

A Prayer for Unity

LORD, I WANT TO BE A GOOD MOTHER.
Sometimes this desire may drive me to put my
children first in ways that are unhealthy. Am I putting
them first to the point that their needs are more
important than my relationship with my spouse?
Do I ever favor a child—even without meaning to—
because I understand them better or because
they are more like me? Please open my eyes to any
priorities that need to change and help me
to wisely steward the relationships of
my children and husband.

Rachel and Leah

COMPETING FOR LOVE

She will never forget the shame of this moment.

Waking up the morning after her marriage to her new husband's look of horror as he realizes he's been tricked into marrying Leah, not Rachel, as he was promised. Leah watches mutely, shame burning her cheeks, as Jacob hastily dresses and rushes out of the room without another word to her. Gathering a blanket around her, she creeps to the doorway where she can overhear the angry, raised voice of Jacob and the cool, consoling voice of her father, Laban.

"What have you done to me?" cries Jacob. "I told you I'd serve you for seven years for *Rachel*, not Leah, and you agreed! Did I not do just that? I'm your nephew and have faithfully worked for you—why have you deceived me?"

Laban sidesteps Jacob's question about motive and matter-of-factly says, "In our country, we do not give the younger daughter in marriage before the firstborn. It is not our custom. I tell you what, complete the week's marriage celebrations with this one, and then I will give you the other one, Rachel, for another seven years of labor."

Leah hears a pause while Jacob considers this counteroffer.

"Fine," Jacob agrees grudgingly.

NOT GOOD ENOUGH

What was supposed to have been Leah's crowning achievement—marriage—was now tainted. Her own father used her to manipulate another seven years of work out of Jacob. And when Jacob turned around and married her younger sister a week after marrying her, I can't help but wonder if Leah was humiliated. It was as if he was proclaiming to the whole world, *Leah's not good enough.*

As we read in the previous chapter, Jacob was on the run from Esau's wrath. He sought refuge with his mother's brother, Laban. There he found herds of sheep and two cousins, Leah and Rachel. When he joined the household, Jacob negotiated with his Uncle Laban for the wages of his labor, and they agreed upon marriage to Rachel after seven years of work. But now the deceiver had gotten a taste of his own medicine. Just as he had tricked his brother out of Isaac's blessing, he was now tricked into marrying a woman he didn't love and locked into seven more years of work.

Scripture is completely silent as to what the circumstances really were concerning Leah's part in her marriage to Jacob. Since Jacob didn't realize he'd been tricked until after the wedding night, it seems like Leah would have known she was a stand-in for her sister, and she clearly didn't reveal herself until the night was over. Was she happy about this because she had no other prospects? Did she love Jacob and want him for herself (she certainly pined for his affection after marriage)? Or was she hurt that her father used her as a pawn to his own advantage? Was she forced by Laban into a charade she had no wish to take part in? Regardless,

Leah would have had no choice but to obey her father. During biblical times "marriages weren't for love but for security and provision."[2] Women did not arrange their own marriages during this period nor was romantic love a major priority. However, Scripture tells us that Rachel was the more beautiful of the two sisters and that Jacob immediately loved her (Gen. 29:16–18). It was Jacob himself who suggested seven years of service for her hand in marriage to his uncle. One would assume Jacob's preference for Rachel was common knowledge to the whole family after Jacob had lived with them for seven years. Or was it a complete secret known only to Laban, giving him the leverage to orchestrate events as he willed? None of these questions can be answered by reading the text. What we *do* know is Leah wanted to be loved by Jacob—and wasn't (Gen. 29:31).

Jealous for Love

But the Lord saw Leah. Like Hagar before her, when everyone else hated Leah, God saw the distress her marriage caused her and sent her the comfort every ancient woman wanted: children. "When the Lord saw that Leah was hated, he opened her womb, but Rachel was barren" (Gen. 29:31). God didn't make Jacob fall in love with Leah. It doesn't seem that anything ever changed in their marriage. But he did act on Leah's behalf and Leah knew it, as we can see from her comments after each child's birth. When Reuben was born she said, "Because the Lord has looked upon my affliction; for now my husband will love me" (Gen. 29:32). When Simeon was born she replied, "Because the Lord has heard that I am hated, he

has given me this son also" (Gen. 29:33). When Levi was born
she said, "Now this time my husband will be attached to me,
because I have borne him three sons" (Gen. 29:34). It's heart-
breaking to read of Leah's longing to be loved and cherished by
Jacob and to know that she did not receive it. However, we see
the progression of Leah's encounter with God in this list. When
she bore her fourth son, Judah, there was no mention of striving
for love anymore. She seemed to cease trying to gain Jacob's
affection through childbirth, at least for a little while. "This time
I will praise the LORD," she declared simply (Gen. 29:35). Then
Leah experienced a period of infertility. Later, she would ask
God to grant her more children and God listened and she bore
two more sons and a daughter.

Despite Leah's jealousy over Jacob's love, which belonged
to her sister, God saw and heard her. It reminds me of Psalm
34:18, which says, "The LORD is near to the brokenhearted and
saves the crushed in spirit." Although Jacob never loved Leah the
way she wanted him to, God planned that the Messiah would
come through her line, not Rachel's. It's Leah's son, Judah, who
will be the one from whom the Lion of Judah comes.

JEALOUS FOR CHILDREN

Rachel seemed to have everything. She had beauty and she
had Jacob's love. But she didn't have children. It was Leah the
unloved who had the children. And Rachel envied her for that.

Rachel had never had any children. Leah had four
successful pregnancies and then ceased to bear any more
babies. Now both sisters began to compete for children through

their servants, Bilhah and Zilpah. Like Sarah who made Hagar
marry Abraham to bear a child in her place, each sister had the
power to give these servant women to Jacob as wives. Bilhah
and Zilpah operated as surrogate mothers so that Jacob gained
four more sons through them. However, the sisters were the
ones who named these children because they were born of
substitute-servant wives. Their children were considered to
"belong" to Leah and Rachel. The names Rachel chose for
Bilhah's children revealed her heart. Of Dan, she said, "God has
judged me, and has also heard my voice and given me a son"
(Gen. 30:6). Of Naphtali, she said, "With mighty wrestlings I
have wrestled with my sister and have prevailed" (Gen. 30:8).
Clearly, Rachel was preoccupied not just with having children
for her own contentment and joy, but with beating out her sister
in some way.

One day during the wheat harvest, Rachel watched as
Reuben made his way back from the fields with a gift of
mandrakes for his mother. Mandrakes are a low-growing
plant with purplish-blue flowers and long taproots that can
sometimes resemble a human body. They are known to be a
sedative and hallucinogen with pain-killing properties and can
be poisonous depending on the quantities ingested. The plant
has also been thought to aid in fertility and to be an aphro-
disiac—which may explain why, when Rachel saw Rueben with
them, she approached Leah.[3]

"Please Leah, may I have some of your son's mandrakes?"
Rachel asked. "You already have my husband's full attention;
would you take my son's mandrakes away too?" Leah responded.
You can almost hear her bitterness in this reply.

Rachel, knowing that Leah was jealous over Jacob's preference for her and that Jacob slept with Rachel most nights, decided to bargain with Leah.

"Well, Jacob may sleep with you tonight if you let me have your son's mandrakes."

Despite Rachel's bargaining for mandrakes and complaining to Jacob directly that if he didn't give her children she would die, it was God who finally "remembered" her and gave her a son, Joseph (Gen. 30:22). With this birth, Rachel proclaimed, "God has taken away my disgrace" (Gen. 30:23 CSB). One can almost hear the joy, relief, and exaltation in this statement. She immediately prayed that God would grant her another son. Indeed, Joseph's name means "He shall add" or "God shall add." Embedded in Joseph's name was a request for more children.

Eventually, five chapters later, God did give Rachel one more son, Benjamin, but that birth would also take her life. Rachel never got to truly experience the satisfaction of enjoying a brood of her own children all around her as Leah did.

Rachel and Leah spent their marriages competing for Jacob's affection through their ability to bear children. Rachel, though loved by Jacob, was anguished over her childlessness and jealous of Leah's growing band of boys. Leah despaired over Jacob's lack of love and tried to gain his affection by the number of children she could produce. To some degree, God gave Rachel and Leah what they wanted, but neither was fully satisfied in God's gifts or the gift of himself. Each wanted what the other had. Where one had beauty and love, she longed for children. Where one had children, she longed for love and affection. Their desire for children was some sort of tug-of-war competition of sisterly rivalry. Their jealous attitudes would then seep into the lives of their children too: just as Leah and Rachel competed with each other for Jacob's affection, so would their children. Their sons would carry their rivalry on, competing for Jacob's fatherly love. And Jacob, in turn, made the same fatal mistake his own father and mother did: by showing favoritism to one child over the others, he set off ill feelings that would threaten to damage his family for years to come.

A LEGACY OF RECONCILIATION

Despite the dysfunction that began in Jacob and Esau's relationship, continued into Leah and Rachel's marriages to Jacob, and then followed into Jacob's relationship with his own sons, the ultimate legacy of Jacob's family is reconciliation and salvation. There are few stories of such complete sibling dysfunction as the story of Joseph and his brothers. This should encourage all of us who have fighting children, whether young or old, that God can redeem all things. Hopefully, very few of us will have children who will actually *sell* their siblings into slavery like Joseph's brothers did!

Eventually, Joseph would change the narrative of his family's pattern of jealousy when he didn't retaliate against the brothers who sold him into slavery, but instead forgave them. Joseph did what his mother was never able to do—he ended the family cycle of competition. He was foreshadowing Christ himself who, though betrayed by his own people and crucified, forgave his fellow man and redeemed us all, giving us the possibility to change our stories too. No matter our family's past failings, God can still use us and change us, which should give every one of us hope when we realize that "This polygamous family, with many shameful things to their credit, was accepted of God, as a whole, to be the beginning of the Twelve Tribes which became the Messianic Nation, chosen by God to bring the Savior into the world."[4] If God used Jacob and his family, he can use our families too.

LEAH AND RACHEL'S GOD ENCOUNTER:

Sisters Rachel and Leah competed for their husband's affection through their ability to bear children. God heard their desire for love and children and answered their prayers, although it was ultimately never enough. Despite the ill feelings that threatened to destroy their family for multiple generations, the legacy of their children was reconciliation and salvation. Rachel's son Joseph modeled Christ-like forgiveness, and the line of the Messiah was established through Leah's son, Judah.

GETTING TO THE HEART

Read Genesis 29–30.

Is there some aspect of competition in your relationships? Do you compete with your family or friends vocationally, financially, or some other way? How can you lay your competition aside?

Do you consider God's gift of himself your greatest gift of all?

Are you satisfied with the good gifts God has given, or are you always discontent? Are there areas where God has answered prayer, like he did with Leah and Rachel's request for children, yet you always demand more?

If there has been competition, hatred, or unforgiveness in your family, how can you follow Joseph's example and leave a legacy of reconciliation? Could such healing start with you?

A Prayer for Reconciliation

LORD, THERE ARE NO PERFECT RELATIONSHIPS. If anything, the Bible proves just that. The founders of our faith lived messed up lives and didn't always follow your will. Despite that, you give grace and hope. Help me not to lead my family in a spirit of unhealthy competition through rivalry or favoritism. Help me not be discontent with the family you've given me. I pray instead that I'd be content with you, Father, the greatest gift of all. Help me seek reconciliation in my family and friendships. It might have to start with me. It might have to start with forgiving past wrongs. Help me be like Joseph and be willing to leave a legacy of forgiveness.

Jochebed

BRAVE TRUST

Jochebed double-checks the papyrus basket she's spent days carefully weaving, making sure it is watertight—every inch thickly covered with a coat of pitch. She has kept her infant son alive these past three months, hidden despite Pharaoh's order to put all male Israelite babies to death. But it is getting harder to keep him a secret any longer, and she has embarked on a perilous plan.

Jochebed tenderly tucks a blanket around her child, who looks up at her with wide-eyed trust. She has already risked much by keeping him alive since birth, but the only chance for his survival is to risk even more! *Will she see him alive again? Will the basket hold? Will it tip, drowning the child in dangerous waters?* Questions play in her mind as she tearfully pushes the basket into the water, while her daughter Miriam watches from a distance, on guard.

Pharaoh's daughter comes down to bathe in the river with her entourage. She spots the basket floating on the water.

"Go, get that basket for me, floating there among the reeds," she directs a servant woman. The woman wades into the water and pushes the floating basket towards the shore, where Pharaoh's daughter stands waiting.

Bending down, she opens the basket, as the sound of crying reaches her ears. With a sharp intake of breath, she sees a baby lying in its floating cradle. Her heart goes out in pity towards the child.

"This is a Hebrew child!" she exclaims.

A young Hebrew girl standing on the bank, previously hidden, parts the rushes and steps forward.

"May I call a Hebrew woman to nurse the child for you?" she asks respectfully.

Pharaoh's daughter looks up, startled.

"Go at once," Pharaoh's daughter commands. Immediately, the girl disappears into the tall reeds.

The girl's feet pound down the path that leads from the water towards a group of Hebrew homes. She bursts into her house calling for her mother.

"What's happened!" cries Jochebed, who has been waiting for news.

"It's okay, he's safe," Miriam says, out of breath. "Pharaoh's daughter has him. She wants you to nurse him!" Miriam clutches her mother's hand and pulls her out of the house and down the path back towards the water.

OUT OF THE WATER

When Pharaoh's daughter discovered the small baby floating amongst the reeds and decided to keep him, Miriam, the baby's sister, stepped in. I used to think Miriam simply did some quick thinking to offer this plan to the Pharaoh's daughter. But now I wonder if her clever mother had already instructed Miriam in what to say. Scripture doesn't tell us, but if Pharaoh's daughter kept a routine and was known to bathe regularly in

the same place at the Nile's edge, Jochebed probably planned
that she would be the one to find him. It was still a risky move.
Pharaoh's daughter could have had as little regard for Hebrew
life as her father. But Jochebed may have been counting on the
other woman to have compassion when faced with a live child
at her mercy. Regardless of these unknowns, Miriam ran off to
fetch a nurse for Moses. Of course, it's Jochebed, the baby's own
mother, that she brought back with her.

I also find myself wondering what kind of woman Pharaoh's
daughter was. Was she married and barren, thus welcoming
a chance to "adopt" a child? Was she single? What did she tell
her father when she came home with a baby—a Hebrew child
at that! Did she have to stand up to her father in order to keep
the child? Or was she the apple of her father's eye, allowed to
do whatever she liked? Was she perceptive enough to know the
nurse was really the baby's mother? I'd wager a guess she did.

The child lived. And it was Pharaoh's daughter who gave
him his name, Moses, meaning "I drew him of the water" (Ex.
2:10). Not only did he live, but he also got to spend more months
or even years with his mother and the rest of his family until
he was weaned. Moses grew up to be an important leader of
the Hebrew nation. Finally, the promise to Abraham and Sarah
was beginning to be fulfilled. Now their descendants were as
numerous as the stars in the sky, but they were slaves to the
Egyptians. Moses was the one chosen by God to lead them into
freedom and their own land promised so long ago to Abraham.
Moses spoke to God in a burning bush, he led them through the
Red Sea that parted on his behalf, and he received the law of
God. The ending was a happy one because Jochebed was willing

to risk so much on behalf of her son. We don't know if she lived to march with him out of slavery. She may have never known the mighty ways that the Lord would one day use him. And not just Moses, but her other children, Aaron and Miriam, also became leaders within the nation of Israel. Her trust in the Lord seemed to have influenced the faith of all her children. But none of these things were yet known to Jochebed as she trusted her son to the Lord's keeping when he was still a baby. His future may have still looked full of peril to Jochebed at that time. Although Moses lived, he was going to live with a king who worshiped pagan gods and wanted him dead. As the adopted son of the most powerful woman in Egypt, his education would be expensive and comprehensive—but pagan. He would be taught that the God of the Israelites was just one god among many, or even worse, that he didn't exist at all. But even in all these details, Jochebed trusted God.

BRAVELY LETTING GO

Jochebed showed bravery, creativity, and trust in a heart-wrenching situation. And although we can clearly see how God sovereignly directed Jochebed's actions, knowing her child would survive and become the leader of the nation of Israel, we're only seeing this after the fact. Jochebed had no idea how it was going to play out. From her perspective, she was just a mother trying to keep her child alive.

Jochebed didn't have the choice to keep Moses in a religious bubble like we may have today. Many Western Christians can choose private Christian education or home education to give their kids a biblical worldview. We have the freedom to choose to only watch faith-based entertainment, listen to Christian music, and block what we don't want our kids to see on the internet. We can buy Christian t-shirts and boycott stores that sell merchandise we think conflicts with our values. Jochebed didn't have these options. Moses would only be under her direct influence for a few brief years. If she wanted her son to live, *he was going to be steeped in pagan culture.*

Jochebed's actions were carefully planned and wise, exhibiting bravery in the face of Pharaoh's orders. But in the end, as her fingers lost their hold on the little basket and it slipped into the water, she had to trust God for the outcome. This was her God-encounter moment. Although we don't hear any mention of God directly speaking to her the way he did to some of our other mothers like Sarah and Hagar, this was the moment she had to trust God with her son's life, physically and spiritually. As his basket floated away, Moses was now literally and figuratively out of her hands.

There's a point in every mother's life when she must do the same. Wisdom and planning are exhausted. The direct influence we once had will dissipate, due to the nature of our children growing up and leaving home. Now there must be a letting go. All that's left is brave and prayerful trust in God, who oversees all situations, no matter how difficult. Whether we have a daughter's mental health crisis to navigate or a son's media habits to pray over, there always comes a point when we've done all we can do, especially as our kids grow older. Now we must wait and see what God will do.

And that takes *brave trust.*

JOCHEBED'S GOD ENCOUNTER:

Jochebed is an amazing model of bravery and trust in God's sovereignty. She carefully and wisely plans a way of escape for her son. She is responsible and dedicated, but ultimately, she has to let go of that tiny waterproof basket carrying her son and trust God's plan for her son's life.

GETTING TO THE HEART

Read Exodus 1–2.

Jochebed defies Pharaoh's orders. She is not arrogant, but humbly and quietly depends on God to direct her steps. Is there an area where you need to take action on behalf of your child in a way that might seem scary or frightening?

Is there an area where you've already done all you can do and now you need to surrender control to God on behalf of your child? This also takes bravery, trust, and dependence. Ask God for this sort of bravery, which often takes a lot of waiting.

A Prayer for Bravery

LORD, SOMETIMES BRAVERY MEANS ACTION,
like when Jochebed has to defy Pharaoh's orders to
keep her son alive. Sometimes bravery is also letting go,
like when Jochebed releases Moses into the care of
a pagan ruler who wants to kill not only her child
but all the male children of her people. Give me the
wisdom to know when each type of bravery
is needed—when to act and when to let go.

Naomi

FROM BITTERNESS TO
A NEW BEGINNING

Nearing Bethlehem, the two women are foot sore and dusty from travel, having set out on their journey days before from Moab. As they approach her former hometown, Naomi feels many emotions swirl within her. It has been ten years since she left Bethlehem. Things were so different then.

Ten years ago times had been hard. But she did not realize then just how good her circumstances were, even during a famine. Ten years ago her husband, Elimelech, and her two fine boys, Mahlon and Chilion, had still been alive. They left Bethlehem during a famine because they heard things were better in Moab. But now she has nothing. No husband, no sons, no home, no wealth. She is destitute, childless, and widowed. It couldn't get much worse.

Well, she has Ruth. At least she isn't *completely* alone.

Naomi tried to convince both daughters-in-law, Ruth and Orpah, to leave her and return to their families, saying, "it is exceedingly bitter to me for your sake that the hand of the LORD has gone out against me" (Ruth 1:13). There was no reason they should suffer with her. They were not Israelites, like she was. They were Moabites. Her sons had married them after they had moved from Bethlehem to Moab. Perhaps that was why God was punishing her family in the first place? Moab had long been one of Israel's enemies. The people of Moab had descended from an incestuous encounter between Lot and his daughter. They worshiped the false god, Chemosh, and in the past had tempted the Israelites to participate in sexual immorality and pagan worship (Num. 25:1–3; Deut. 23:3–6). Maybe all this calamity was punishment for living among those who didn't acknowledge Yahweh? Naomi didn't know. It didn't really matter anymore anyway.

Although she wept, Orpah listened to Naomi's advice and returned to her own family. But Ruth wouldn't budge.

"Where you go I will go, and where you lodge I will lodge. Your people shall be my people, and your God my God. Where you die I will die, and there will I be buried," Ruth had said through tears, clinging to Naomi (Ruth 1:16–17). Naomi reluctantly gave in. What could she do anyway? She didn't have the strength to resist Ruth, and to be honest, she welcomed the company.

That had been several days ago. Now, Naomi looks around as they enter Bethlehem, taking in the changes as she feels eyes turn towards her. Curious faces look up from tasks and lean out of windows and doorways. Some she recognizes and others she does not.

"Naomi, is that you?" A woman approaches her questioningly—her once-familiar face has aged, probably just like her own. A murmuring begins to echo from house to house as Naomi hears whispers and exclamations:

"It's Naomi!"

"Naomi is back! Who is that with her?"

As her former friends and townspeople begin to gather around her, Naomi feels all of her various emotions coalesce into intense bitterness. This was not the way she'd wanted to return.

"Don't call me Naomi," she snaps at those nearest her. "Call me Mara, for the Almighty has made my life very bitter. I went away full, but the LORD has brought me back empty. Why call me Naomi? The LORD has afflicted me; the Almighty has brought misfortune upon me" (Ruth 1:20–21 NIV).

As she stands in the center of town, the irony of her life seems to laugh in her face. She'd left this town called Bethlehem, which means "house of bread" during a famine to find bread elsewhere. They had left Bethlehem so they wouldn't die, yet all had died except Naomi. And now she is returning more destitute than she'd left. She is returning to "the house of bread" to seek out sustenance once again. But she is no longer the woman she'd once been. She is no longer Naomi, meaning pleasant. No, she is now Mara, meaning bitter. And she fully embraces this new identity. Wasn't it the Lord himself who had changed her from pleasant to bitter?

THE HOUSE OF BREAD

They needed food. That much was certain. Bethlehem, the house of bread, needed to provide them with grain. And thankfully, they had returned at the beginning of the barley harvest. Early one morning Ruth set out in search of a field to glean in. Israel's law provided that the edges of fields were not to be completely reaped so that poor people like foreigners or widows could glean from them. Now, Naomi was waiting for Ruth to return home. She looked up as she heard someone approaching.

"Look what I've got!" exclaimed Ruth, rushing through the door despite her weariness from a full day's back-bending work in the field. "An ephah of barley—enough for about two weeks!" she proclaimed proudly. "And I even saved you some leftover food from my midday meal," she said, searching for the leftovers that she had carefully packed and saved.

Naomi's heart soared in sudden thankfulness. "Where did you glean today?" she asked, reaching out to touch the barley and feel it slide through her fingers.

"I happened to work in a field today owned by a man named Boaz," replied Ruth. "He told me not to glean in any other fields but his, and he would make sure I was safe. He even shared his bread and wine with me!"

"May he be blessed by the Lord!" Naomi exclaimed, suddenly recognizing Boaz's name. "Boaz is one of our relatives, one of our kinsman redeemers!" Hope suddenly soared into Naomi's heart for the first time since returning to Israel.

A BOLD PROPOSAL

A redeemer in the Bible could provide for two types of "redemption." A relative could redeem property that was being sold so that it could stay within the family line (Lev. 25:25–28). Another form of redemption was when a man would marry his brother's childless widow in order to provide an heir on behalf of the dead husband, so that his lineage would not end (Deut. 25:5–9). This is what was called a "levirate marriage"—the firstborn son from this union would be considered the dead husband's offspring and would receive his inheritance.

Naomi knew all this, and for the first time she realized there was hope for her future—both for her *and* Ruth. Now that the barley and wheat harvests were almost over, she hatched a plan. She told Ruth to make herself attractive and to head down to the threshing floor where Boaz and his men were working. She instructed Ruth to wait until the men had finished eating and drinking and fallen asleep, and then to go to where Boaz was sleeping and to uncover his feet and lie down. Ruth seemed to trust her mother-in-law implicitly and without question said, "All that you say I will do."

Boaz was startled awake in the middle of the night. Disoriented and confused, he realized there was a woman lying at his feet!

"Who are you?" he whispered, trying not to awaken the other sleeping men around him.

"It's Ruth," Ruth whispered back. "Take me under your protection. You're my close relative, you're my kinsman redeemer—you have the right to marry me."

This is a confusing part of the story to modern readers, but basically Ruth was claiming Boaz as her redeemer and asking him to marry her. It's unclear why Naomi instructed Ruth to sneak onto the threshing floor and uncover Boaz's feet in the middle of the night instead of approaching him directly. Although it was not traditional or proper for a woman to approach a man with a marriage proposal, it seems even stranger to do it in the middle of the night. But perhaps under the cover of night was really the only way this conversation could take place without encouraging interest and gossip from others. Boaz was not put off by Ruth's approach; instead, he complimented her for not chasing after younger men. He agreed to do what she asked but told her there was one problem: there was someone else who was an even closer redeemer to her than he was. He told her not to worry; he would sort it out in the morning.

Before dawn, Boaz discretely sent Ruth home with more barley as a sign of his willingness to fulfill her request.

THE KINSMAN REDEEMER

Boaz immediately headed to the town gate the morning after Ruth's night-time visit. In those days, this was where business was conducted by the men of the town. Soon, the man who was the closer relation came by, and Boaz stopped him to explain that he had the opportunity to redeem some land. At first, the man was eager to redeem the land—until he found out Ruth came with it! Then he quickly backtracked, concerned that if he were to do so, it would mess up the inheritance in his own family line. So, the men agreed, with ten city elders as witnesses, that Boaz would be the one to redeem both the land and Ruth and provide an heir in the name of her deceased husband, Mahlon.

The elders and all the people who witnessed the agreement blessed Boaz and Ruth and mentioned two other women we've already met: Rachel and Leah. Remember, Rachel and Leah were instrumental in establishing the twelve tribes of Israel. They were "founding mothers" and their names were evoked to speak a blessing over Ruth's life in hopes that she too would build up Israel with her offspring. Little did they know what an important offspring she would bear.

NO LONGER BITTER, BUT BLESSED

Often, the emphasis of the book of Ruth is the love story between Boaz and Ruth. But as the book concludes, the focus shifts back to the woman whose voice we first heard at the beginning of this tale: Naomi.

It's not Ruth we find holding the newborn baby boy born to Boaz and Ruth, but Naomi. The townswomen crowd around Naomi once again, and this time she doesn't meet them with bitterness. Instead, she accepts the blessing they speak over her in her old age, "The women said to Naomi, 'Blessed be the LORD, who has not left you without a family redeemer today. May his name become well known in Israel. He will renew your life and sustain you in your old age. Indeed, your daughter-in-law, who loves you and is better to you than seven sons, has given birth to him'" (Ruth 4:14–15 CSB). In this last scene, we see Naomi basking in the blessing of a new beginning, with Obed—the father of Jesse, who in turn will become the father of King David—on her lap.

OUR KINSMAN REDEEMER

Like Jochebed, Naomi seemingly has no direct interaction with God. We don't hear her praying like Hannah, whom we'll meet in the next chapter, and no voice speaks directly to her as God did to Hagar. Yet God has a new beginning planned for Naomi, one she couldn't have imagined if she tried. Because Naomi turns around and goes back to Bethlehem, her legacy trickles down to those of us who follow Christ.

At first it seems like Naomi does everything wrong. She left

Israel to live with the enemy. Her sons married Moabite women who were pagan worshipers. She vocalized her bitterness for all to hear. But God literally redeemed her life—he didn't erase her loss or pain but used it in a way to make his plans go forward. Her willingness to go back to her hometown, seemingly defeated, set in motion all the good that would come to her in her future.

Sometimes it's hard to go back, but sometimes it's the right thing to do. Sometimes it feels like the opposite of progress to return to our hometown, a former job, or a church we'd left. Naomi left the land of the pagans and went back to God's people. Even if Naomi had remained faithful to the Lord for the ten years she lived in Moab—and it seems like she probably did, since Ruth knew all about Naomi's God—it was not the place that held a future for her. At first it seemed like her soul was still disgruntled, considering her bitter spirit, but at some point, there was a turn. The bitterness began to dissipate. At some point she recognized God had been providing for her all along: through Ruth as a faithful companion, in the provision of grain gathered by hard work, and through Boaz, their kinsman redeemer.

Amazingly, God used Naomi's *return* to Israel to *redeem* Israel—and not just Israel—but the whole world through our ultimate Kinsman Redeemer, Jesus the Messiah. And God didn't use perfect, pure-blooded Israelites in Jesus' family line. He used Boaz, son of Rahab, the Canaanite prostitute who was grafted into God's family and Ruth, a Moabite outsider (Matt. 1:5). It doesn't matter what our family history or past looks like if we, like Naomi, turn to our Kinsman Redeemer Jesus. We too need redemption, which Jesus provides: "In him we have redemption through his blood, the forgiveness of sins, in accordance with the riches of God's grace that he lavished on us" (Eph. 1:7–8 NIV). Like Naomi, we need spiritual nourishment and sustenance: "I am the bread of life. Whoever comes to me will never go hungry, and whoever believes in me will never be thirsty" (John 6:35 NIV). Jesus has provided for all of our needs, because Jesus is our Kinsman Redeemer.

NAOMI'S GOD ENCOUNTER:

Naomi returned to her hometown of Bethlehem in a state of bitter grief. It's not hard to understand why. She was destitute, childless, and widowed. But God had a new beginning planned for Naomi, one of redemption not just for her but for all of us.

GETTING TO THE HEART

Read Ruth 1–4.

Are there any places in your life where you've left the Lord to go live in a pagan land? Do you need to return to a spiritual heritage you've left behind? If this is true, pray to be brave enough to recognize it and be bold enough to turn around.

Is there any bitterness in your life that you need to give to God? He is already willing to be your Kinsman Redeemer and he is willing to give you a new beginning. He won't erase past losses but he's willing to give you a fresh start. Maybe you need to come to him for the first time—or the hundredth time—but he's always willing to take your bitterness on himself if you let him.

A Prayer for New Beginnings

LORD, I'VE MESSED UP.
There are things that I regret doing,
places I regret going. Sometimes the consequences
of my own wrong actions I blame on you. But you are
always willing to make me new, to redeem my past and
give me a new beginning if I turn from sin and accept
you as my Savior and my Kinsman Redeemer. Heal me
from any bitterness I'm still hanging onto and help me
follow you because you are the Bread of Life.
Without you the path always leads to death,
but with you there is hope of new life,
both in this life and the one to come.

Hannah

A WOMAN OF PRAYER

She's oblivious to all that is around her. Weeping and desperate to be alone, away from the provoking and cruel words of Peninnah, Hannah rushes up the path to the tabernacle to pour out her heart in prayer.

It was like this every year. Every year they left their hometown of Ramah in the hill country of Ephraim and traveled the fifteen miles north to worship and offer sacrifices at Shiloh.[5] And every year Peninnah—who was the other wife of Hannah's husband—took her snide verbal assaults up a notch. Her attacks were so provoking that Hannah no longer had the strength to eat. All Hannah wanted to do was cry. And why was Hannah in all this misery? Because Hannah was barren. Hannah's husband, Elkanah, is sympathetic and doesn't blame Hannah for her barrenness, which could have been viewed as a symbol of disgrace in ancient culture. Instead, he gives her a "double portion" from the animal they sacrificed at the tabernacle. Perhaps this made Peninnah jealous of Elkanah's love and affection despite the fact she was the one with the children? Since Hannah is named first as Elkanah's wife, it is a possibility that he only married Peninnah in order to have an heir once it became clear Hannah wasn't conceiving. We don't know the details, but like Leah and Rachel, adding a second wife didn't bode well for domestic happiness.

Hannah can't endure the verbal torture anymore. Something has to change. She hurries past the old priest, Eli, who is leaning against the doorpost of the tabernacle, and enters the holy structure. Once in the house of worship, Hannah prays in desperation to the Lord. She also makes a vow, and a vow is no small thing.

"Lord, if you give me a son, I will give him back to you for all the days of his life and no razor shall touch his head," she whispers hoarsely into the silence of the tabernacle.

A vow means serious business in biblical times. Hannah's vow reveals the purity of her heart's desire. Not only does she want a son, but she is also willing to give him up. The mention of no razor touching his head seems to be a reference to making a Nazirite vow, although she doesn't mention the other facets of the Nazirite vow laid out in Numbers 6:1–9, like abstaining from alcohol. Also, Leviticus 27:1–8 mentions that a child as young as a month old could be vowed to the Lord to be set apart for service in the temple. Hannah clearly intends for her would-be-son to be dedicated to the Lord's work for his entire life.

One son. That's all she wants, and then she'll give him up. I don't know if I could make a vow like that. Could you?

Suddenly, Hannah's fervent concentration is broken by a stern voice.

"How long will you continue being drunk? Stop drinking wine!" It is Eli, the high priest. Even in the tabernacle she is not left alone, but falsely accused and misunderstood. Is there no peace for her even in this place of worship?

Eli's words reveal the depraved state of the tabernacle under his leadership. His sons, Hophni and Phinehas, are described as worthless men that do not know the Lord (1 Sam. 2:12). They abuse and bully worshipers in their roles as priests, instead of viewing their role as a gift (Num. 18:7). They forcibly take the best portions of people's meat offerings for themselves and conduct inappropriate sexual relationships with women who are supposed to be serving at the tabernacle. Although Eli doesn't approve of their actions, he only confronts them verbally and takes no strong steps to stop their behavior. As Gien Karssen writes in her book, *Her Name is Woman*, "The priest who hadn't dared deal harshly with his own sons felt no reservation in dealing with Hannah. The old man revealed a lack of insight and poor self-control. His words also revealed that in those days drunk people and bad women were not an unusual sight in the house of God. Even Eli's own sons slept with the women who gathered at the door of the tabernacle."[6] Eli doesn't even recognize private prayer when he sees it. But despite his slander, Hannah responds to him with grace, explaining that she is very "troubled in spirit" and had been in prayer. She is no drunken woman.

Eli realizes his mistake and blesses her: "Go in peace and may the God of Israel answer the request you have made to him."

Hannah dries her eyes and leaves the Lord's house. Breathing deeply, she knows she must face Peninnah again, but she now has the fortitude to deal with it. She leaves her burden behind her at the tabernacle and finally feels peace and contentment. She is also ravenous, so she goes back to her tent to eat.

DEDICATED TO THE LORD

Eventually, Hannah conceived a son. Can you imagine her joy as she feels the first kick? Or her gratitude as her belly became swollen with the son of her prayers?

At long last, her son was born and named Samuel, which means "name of God" or "heard of God." I'm sure Hannah relished each moment with him as he grew from a baby into a toddler. It wasn't until he was weaned (which often was between two and three years old) that she journeyed with him to the tabernacle to dedicate him to the Lord and leave him in Eli's care.

The fact that Elkanah did not override Hannah's vow showed his love and respect for her. We already know he favored her as his wife and didn't blame her for her childless state, but he also respected her vow to the Lord. Elkanah was not part of the decision to make a vow concerning their first-born son, and he could have been angry or refused to honor it. Numbers 30:6–8 provided a provision for a husband to cancel his wife's vow, but Elkanah did not do that. Instead, he honored and even confirmed it when he told her, "Do what seems best to you; wait until you have weaned him; only, may the Lord establish his word" (1 Sam. 1:23). Elkanah supported Hannah's vow despite the fact it would mean giving up his son.

Hannah's dedication of Samuel at the tabernacle exemplified her trust and faith in God. Eli had already raised two sons who were uncontrollably corrupt. How could she trust this man with the precious son that she had so desperately prayed for? Like Jochebed before her, she trusted her young son to God amid an environment of corruption. But unlike Jochebed, she'd had a choice in the matter. She *chose* to dedicate Samuel to the Lord's service; it hadn't been a life-or-death situation. In some ways this situation was almost worse, because these men weren't "pagans" but instead priests who were misusing their authority in the name of God. One might assume that in the midst of such debauchery, Samuel would grow up tainted by their influence.

But Hannah knew God heard prayers. This had already been proven. And as she dedicated Samuel to the Lord's service, she prayed one of the most beautiful prayers in all of Scripture, foreshadowing Mary's Magnificat in the New Testament:

> My heart rejoices in the LORD;
> in the LORD my horn is lifted high.
> My mouth boasts over my enemies,
> for I delight in your deliverance.
> There is no one holy like the LORD;
> there is no one besides you;
> there is no Rock like our God.
> Do not keep talking so proudly
> or let your mouth speak such arrogance,
> for the LORD is a God who knows,
>   and by him deeds are weighed.
> The bows of the warriors are broken,
>   but those who stumbled are armed with strength.
> Those who were full hire themselves out for food,
>   but those who were hungry are hungry no more.
> She who was barren has borne seven children,
>   but she who has had many sons pines away.

The LORD brings death and makes alive;
he brings down to the grave and raises up.
The LORD sends poverty and wealth;
    he humbles and he exalts.
He raises the poor from the dust
    and lifts the needy from the ash heap;
he seats them with princes
    and has them inherit a throne of honor.
For the foundations of the earth are the LORD'S;
    on them he has set the world.
He will guard the feet of his faithful servants,
    but the wicked will be silenced in the place of
    darkness.
It is not by strength that one prevails;
    those who oppose the LORD will be broken.
The Most High will thunder from heaven;
    the LORD will judge the ends of the earth.
He will give strength to his king
    and exalt the horn of his anointed.
(1 Samuel 2:1–10 NIV)

Her prayer showed utter confidence in the Lord as she exulted in the Lord's strength and sovereignty over the righteous and the unrighteous, the humble and the proud. And in the years to come, as she sewed Samuel a new little robe each year to give him when they went to the tabernacle, that prayer must have echoed in her heart. With each stitch a prayer for him was on her lips.

Hannah's prayer connected to Jesus Christ's future kingship in a significant way when she said, "He [the Lord] will give strength to his king and exalt the power of his anointed." There was not yet a king in Israel. Saul and David were yet to be born and Israel had not demanded one, but Hannah referred to a king, calling him *his anointed*. In Hebrew, the word here for "anointed" means "a consecrated person" such as a king or priest, or more specifically, "Messiah."[7] Not only did her hymn prophetically look forward to Israel's earthly kingship but also the heavenly one, established by Jesus.

God's blessings for Hannah did not end with Samuel. Hannah went on to bear three more sons and two daughters. She would no longer be the childless subject of Peninnah's cruel insults.

And Samuel? What happened to child of Hannah's prayers? He became the last judge of Israel and a God-fearing prophet who leads Israel towards righteousness, the complete opposite legacy of Eli's sons.

Prayer defined Hannah's life. In two short chapters in the Bible, Hannah prayed with such raw emotion, desperation and joy, that one can only imagine the depth of her love for the Lord. She turned to God in her darkest hour, and once that hour is passed, she turned again to him in her deepest joy. Hannah encountered God through her circumstances by coming to him in prayer. She could have let her circumstances drive her *away* from God in bitterness, but instead, her circumstances became the vehicle that drove her *towards* God.

My prayers seem shallow in comparison to Hannah's. They seem lame and tepid. I want to learn from Hannah's specific and bold example in prayer. She didn't rely on herself to raise a faithful son, but instead relied on God's sustaining sovereignty even when Samuel was living amid corrupt religious leaders. I want to pray and praise as fervently as she did when my kids also face similar circumstances at school, with their friends, or yes, even at church. I want to faithfully pray for my children as Hannah prayed for Samuel, both before and after he was born. To not only remember—but to act on the promise that the prayers of a righteous person are powerful and effective (James 5:16 NIV).

HANNAH'S GOD ENCOUNTER:

Hannah prayed one of the most amazing and sacrificial prayers in Scripture. Her obvious fervency even brought a rebuke from Eli, Israel's dubious high priest. Hannah encountered and interacted with God through prayer and showed us what it means to have a life characterized by passionate prayer and reliance on God's protection for her son.

GETTING TO THE HEART

Read 1 Samuel 1:1–2:21.

Hannah took her despair over her infertility directly to the Lord. Do you take your requests to the Lord or do you scheme and manipulate to get your way like Sarah, Rachel, and Leah did?

Can you be bolder and more specific in your times of prayer with God?

Our kids will face corruption in the world. Are you praying for God to sustain them—or do you believe that it's all up to you?

Do you remember to thank and praise God when you see answered prayers in your life or the life of your children?

A Prayer for Help to Pray

LORD, I ADMIT
I often don't come to you in prayer.
Busy and preoccupied, I often rely on
my own strength, solutions, and wisdom.
Help me learn from Hannah's life and seek to
encounter you in and through prayer. Help me come
to you with my needs and desires as well as those of my
children. Help me trust you with my kids. I know you
love them even more than I do and that they are safe
in your hands. Help me thank you when you meet my
needs and answer my prayers. I know you are always
eager to be in communication with me. Help me take
advantage of the awesome privilege that we have
as New Testament Christians to come to you
with no other mediator than Christ.

Bathsheba

FROM DEVASTATION TO REDEMPTION

It is a beautiful spring evening. Bathsheba is dutifully fulfilling God's law by purifying herself after seven days of uncleanliness due to her period, just as Leviticus 15:19 instructed. Her husband, Uriah, is away at war with the Ammonites. He is one of King David's "mighty men," a kind of special forces known for their feats of strength and valor within the king's army.

Bathsheba finishes bathing and settles down for a quiet evening, only to be startled by a sharp knock at her door.

She is not expecting anyone. Curious, she opens the door and peers out into the street. Several messengers dressed in royal attire stand before her. Sudden panic grips her. Were they there to announce that Uriah has been killed in battle?

"Yes?" she tries to not let fear shake her voice.

"Bathsheba, wife of Uriah?" asks the one who seems to be in charge.

"Yes, I am she," says Bathsheba.

"You've been summoned to the palace. Please come with us," the messenger commands.

"Yes, of course, but do you know why?" Bathsheba asks, still concerned. She can only think that something must have happened to Uriah.

"No, we have no other message than that you are to come to the palace at once."

"Of course," Bathsheba says. One couldn't say no to the king or keep him waiting. Maybe it concerned her grandfather, Ahithophel, one of David's most honored and revered advisors at court. Could he be ill? She would find out soon enough. Trying to keep her worries under control, Bathsheba quickly follows King David's messengers as they make their way toward the palace.

She had never noticed King David on the rooftop of his palace, watching her while she bathed.

. . .

There is no doubt about it. She is pregnant. She feels sick to her stomach, and not just due to the baby. What should she do? What *could* she do? She is pregnant with King David's child, and she feels powerless, just as she had felt when she arrived at the palace. At first the king had feigned interest in Uriah's welfare on the battlefield. But he soon made no secret of his ulterior motives for summoning her. What choice did she have, in the presence of a king whose every command is obeyed? Now she would pay the humiliating price.

What would Uriah do when he found out? She trembles at the thought, tears stinging her eyes. Uriah is a good man, honest and brave. He would feel betrayed, both by the king he is fighting for, and by his wife.

There is only one thing she can do. She sends a message to the king. It is his mess to clean up.

. . .

Uriah had come home but she had not seen him. And now he is dead.

Uriah had considered himself still on duty when he was called to the palace from his place in the army besieging the city of Rabbah. He had feasted with King David, so Bathsheba had heard. But he had not come to see her. Unknowingly, he had denied her one last time to be with him. Unknowingly, he had failed to save her from a future humiliation she'd been desperate for him to protect her from. Now he is dead, killed on the front lines of battle. Everyone knew Uriah did not visit her on his trip back home. Is she now to bear the humiliation of being known as an adulteress while David continues living in his palace with no consequences? The penalty for adultery is death. But no one knew she'd been with David except for the palace servants. Surely they would keep their mouths shut—or only gossip amongst themselves.

Bathsheba grieves deeply over her husband and everything that has happened to her. When her seven days of ritual mourning have passed, there is another knock on her door. Palace messengers have come for her once again.

"We've been sent to bring you to the palace," a messenger says. "You are to bring anything of personal value with you."

"I need time to gather up my things!" Bathsheba exclaims.

"We have been instructed to wait and help transport anything you need to take with you," the messenger replies.

Bathsheba scans the home she's shared with Uriah, considering what from her old life she wants to bring to the palace. Some semblance of relief flows through her. At least now the child growing within her would not grow up a bastard. At least now she won't die. At least she is spared that.

VIXEN OR INNOCENT VICTIM?

Bathsheba is often framed as a temptress and an adulteress. I've heard more than one message that paints her in that light. David sinned ... but Bathsheba tempted him. However, Scripture frames David as the offender. In the time of year when kings go to battle, he is lounging on his couch (2 Sam. 11:1). Instead of battling the Ammonites alongside his men, he seemingly has nothing better to do but walk aimlessly on his roof. From the beginning of this narrative in 2 Samuel 11, the author sets us up to see that David is failing as a king. He is not the type of leader he used to be.

He saw Bathsheba and stared. But it didn't stop there—he wanted her. Finding out who she was should have stopped him in his tracks. She was a married woman—married to one of his mighty men, no less! Uriah was part of his inner circle of warriors, a man David would have known personally. A man who was risking his life on behalf of his country and king.

Bathsheba was also the daughter of Eliam—likely the same Eliam listed in 2 Samuel 23:34 as another one of David's mighty men. That meant her grandfather was Ahithophel, one of David's chief counselors (2 Sam. 16:23). She was not a nobody: every man in her life had an important role in service to their king. But David took advantage of her unprotected status and summoned her to the palace. The description of the crime is devastatingly spare: "So David sent messengers and took her, and she came to him, and he lay with her" (2 Sam. 11:4).

We don't know what went on between them besides the fact that David had sex with her. The language is not as clear as other passages that describe rape (like the stories of Dinah and Tamar) and has been argued in different ways. Some argue that David raped Bathsheba, while others claim that she was a consenting participant. In the original Hebrew, the "word for 'took' can refer to merely acquiring something or to actually taking it by force."[8] The Hebrew word for "lay" has sexual connotations.[9] If we look at the broader definitions described in Scripture, we see that in biblical times, the punishment for what we would call consensual adultery was the death penalty. "If a man commits adultery with a married woman—if he commits adultery with his neighbor's wife—both the adulterer and the adulteress must be put to death" (Lev. 20:10 CSB). But the law also established that in the context of rape, only the rapist would deserve capital punishment: "But if the man encounters an engaged woman in the open country, and he seizes and rapes her, only the man who raped her must die. Do nothing to the young woman, because she is not guilty of an offense deserving death. This case is just like one in which a man attacks his neighbor and murders him" (Deut. 22:25–26 CSB). One thing is clear: Bathsheba had no legal recourse to resist. Although there was a law in place to protect her, and the law was clear that the punishment for rape and adultery was death, the king *was* the law. How could she appeal to the law when the king was the very one flouting it? As Tara-Leigh Cobble puts it, "She can't appeal to the law, because the king is her offender."[10] No one was higher than the king—except God.

And we're told God was not happy with David.

Other details of the context of this story suggest that Bathsheba is innocent as well. When Bathsheba is described as bathing, the author makes a point of clarifying the purpose of her bathing. She is simply obeying the law by performing ritual cleansing after her period; there is no suggestion of enticement or exhibitionism.

Then David sinks deeper into sin, trying to cover his actions. Once he knows Bathsheba is pregnant, he sends for Uriah in hopes that Uriah will sleep with Bathsheba so there would be no reason to suspect that she is pregnant with another man's child. However, men who were engaged in combat were supposed to forgo sexual activity since it was ritually impure, and Uriah reminds David of that (1 Sam. 21:5). Undeterred, David tries to get him drunk and send him home again, but it still doesn't work. David then resorts to murdering one of his best fighters: in a scene as dramatic and ironic as a Shakespearean tragedy, Uriah returns to the battlefield bearing a letter that seals his own fate.

Bathsheba's innocence is also implied in the way the prophet Nathan holds David solely responsible for what has happened. When he confronts David, he tells a parable, casting Bathsheba in the innocent role of a "little ewe lamb." And finally, the Bible refers to Bathsheba as "Uriah's wife" even after she is married to David, reminding us further still of David's abuse of power (2 Sam. 12:15; Matt. 1:6). If Bathsheba had been an equal partner in sinful enticement or consensual adultery, we could expect Scripture to hold her responsible. Given all of this context, it would seem Bathsheba is not the one to blame in this episode from David's life.

GOD IS BIG ENOUGH

Whether you view David's sin as adultery or rape, Scripture puts the blame squarely on David. And David should have been put to death for his actions, both according to Deuteronomy 22:25-29 (which outlines the punishment for rape) and Leviticus 20:10 (which outlines the punishment for adultery). If it is consensual adultery, then Bathsheba should have been put to death, too—in which case it would be strange for a prophet of God to portray her as a "little ewe lamb," if she was a willing and sinful participant. So why does Bathsheba get blamed sometimes?

I wonder if we struggle to interpret this story rightly because we can't reconcile the tension between David as "a man after God's own heart" (1 Sam. 13:14) and David as a selfish king who commits sexual immorality and murder. We like the testimonies that are clear cut: "I used to be a drug addict, addicted to porn, had an affair, but *then* I became a Christian, and I never did any of that again." These are the victorious stories we like to hear. And once we know Christ, we *should* be on a path toward holiness, but we are still sinners. Scripture doesn't have a problem with sharing the unvarnished truth that we don't want to hear: David knew God and blatantly sinned anyway.

David is so often portrayed as the hero in our Bible stories. We like David. He defeats Goliath. He writes songs and sings them while dodging Saul's spears. He refuses to kill Saul when he has a chance. We can't wrap our head around what goes wrong. But what if David isn't the hero after all? What if God is the hero? If we believe the good news that God's grace is sufficient for salvation, why do we act like it's not sufficient after the first time we come to God, when we belong to him and yet still sin? Do we believe grace is a one-time deal? David knew God when he committed his most reprehensible acts and attempted to cover them up.

But God is big enough to deal with sexual sin. He sees it. He knows it. He isn't afraid to call it out. And he can forgive it too. But first we must stop hiding it and bring it into the open like Proverbs 28:13 says: "Whoever conceals their sins does not prosper, but the one who confesses and renounces them finds mercy" (CSB). Mercy is waiting for the one who honestly reveals his own sin instead of hiding it until someone else finds out. It's the sufficiency of God's grace that should give us the strength to come clean. We can't hide our sin from God, nor should we hide it from others who need to know. And if our sin is found out and brought into the light by someone else, like Nathan did for David, let's own it like David finally did when he admitted, "I have sinned against the Lord." It is this honest response that makes David a man after God's own heart. David eventually owned what he did with no other qualifying comments and that was what was needed: repentance. David, as the perpetrator, is not let off the hook. He is confronted and he responds. He is forgiven, but his crime still demands consequences. Perhaps this is the ancient lesson David's story teaches us.

FORGIVEN . . . BUT
CONSEQUENCES REMAIN

David's sin was forgiven, and Nathan told him he wouldn't die as punishment like he should. But there would still be consequences. First, David was told that the sword would never depart from his house, indicating a future of violent deaths within his family—the most immediate death would be that of the child born of his sin with Bathsheba. And secondly, while David had violated Bathsheba in secret, his wives would one day be violated publicly, on a rooftop for all Israel to see, by his son Absalom, who was seeking to take David's throne. Most ironic of all, the mastermind of this plan would be David's once-trusted advisor, Ahithophel, most likely Bathsheba's grandfather. Was this a personal payback for what David had done to Ahithophel's granddaughter? We'll never know.

But we can't lose sight of Bathsheba in the midst of David's repentance and consequences. And if we're honest, it seems like she gets a raw deal here. Her husband is killed, and she then must marry her violator, her husband's murderer. After all that, the child (by all indications, her firstborn) dies. This new mother suffers the devastation of losing her baby as a consequence for another's sin—a sin that she had no power to stop.

What was Bathsheba thinking or feeling? Did she hate David for a time? Was she angry at God for the death of her child? Unlike many of the mothers we've looked at in this book, we have no words from her until she is much older. We don't overhear her prayers like we do Hannah's. We don't hear her complaints for children and affection like we do from Rachel and Leah. We don't see her change from bitter to blessed like Naomi.

But we do see her one more time in Scripture.

DEVASTATION REDEEMED

Bathsheba had four sons by David, and Solomon was one of them (1 Chron. 3:5). And it says the Lord loved him (2 Sam. 12:24). The Lord's favor rested on Bathsheba's son who, like Jacob, would inherit the family blessing—in this case, the kingdom—even though he was not the firstborn son. Although David had made known his desire for Solomon to reign after him, a battle between brothers ensued.

Bathsheba, now years older, was the one the prophet Nathan turned to for support in getting Solomon his rightful kingdom. They worked together to approach an old and dying King David and reminded him of what he promised. And when David eventually died, Solomon took the throne. He respected his mother so much that he, the king, "stood up to greet her, bowed to her, sat down on his throne, and had a throne placed for the king's mother. So she sat down at his right hand" (1 Kings 2:19 CSB). This is where we last see Bathsheba in the narrative: enthroned with her son. The woman once humiliated, disgraced, and sinned against had the joy of experiencing her son's love and respect and seeing him crowned king. She became the mother of the wisest king in history. Perhaps it was her influence in raising him that caused him to cherish wisdom and knowledge and ask God for it over possessions, wealth, or honor (2 Chron. 1:10–12).

Little did she know that another king would come through her family line. A greater king. One who would not commit the sins of David and Solomon but would redeem them. One who would redeem the sins that had been committed against Bathsheba herself.

The last place Bathsheba is mentioned in the Bible is in the genealogy of Christ, in the book of Matthew, though she is not mentioned by name. Instead, the Bible reminds us that God did not forget what Bathsheba endured before becoming the mother of Solomon. Even though she was legitimately married to David when Solomon was born, Matthew lists her as "the wife of Uriah" (Matt. 1:6). Despite her humiliation and pain, God planned for Bathsheba to be part of the earthly lineage of his own son, Jesus.

No matter what shame or grief women suffer at the hands of others, God still offers redemption and hope. Bathsheba's God-encounter doesn't seem to appear in her lifetime. It happens when she's long gone. In this genealogy of Christ, it's not Sarah, Rebekah, or Leah who are recognized, but the women whose stories could have been swept under the rug. It's the mothers who had a past, whether by their own doing or the doing of others. It's Tamar, Rahab, Ruth, and Bathsheba who are included.

Tamar tricks her father-in-law into sleeping with her when he dishonors her by not fulfilling his responsibilities towards her after the death of her husband. Rahab, a Canaanite, lives a life of prostitution before being grafted into the life of Israel. Ruth, a Moabite, is from a people group who were enemies of Israel. Then we are reminded of Bathsheba, who had rightly been Uriah's wife—a woman who had little control over the events that moved her into the palace of King David. In his genealogy, Matthew

> gives the church four new matriarchs, and all of them preach the gospel of the deep and wide mercy of God. These four scandals in their way preach the gospel of divine mercy, which is Matthew's whole mission to proclaim. Matthew will later teach us that Jesus came "not for the righteous, but *for sinners*" (Matt 9:13); but already in his genealogy Matthew is teaching us that Jesus came not only *for*, but *through*, sinners. God did not begin to stoop into our sordid human story at Christmas only; he was stooping all the way through the Old Testament.[11]

Bathsheba's inclusion in the genealogy of Jesus gives her a position of honor and recognition. And this reminds us that God can take our deepest shame, our most devastating life circumstances, and redeem them for his kingdom purposes. We don't have to have a perfect story to be used by God.

BATHSHEBA'S GOD ENCOUNTER:

After being used as a pawn to satisfy David's lust, grieving the murder of her husband and the subsequent death of her child, Bathsheba faced a bleak future. Despite her humiliation, God planned for her to be part of the earthly lineage of his own son, Jesus. No matter what shame or grief women suffer, God still offers redemption and hope.

GETTING TO THE HEART

Read 2 Samuel 11–12; 1 Kings 1–2; Matthew 1:6.

If you were sinned against sexually, do you still internalize shame over it? Can you trust that God loves you no matter what has happened to you?

If you've experienced an abortion, rape, or other traumatic events that may or may not have been under your control, can you give your emotional wounds to God for healing? (Consider counseling or therapy to work through these memories in the healthiest way possible. And if a crime has been committed against you, please consider telling a trusted individual and seeking the legal, spiritual, and/or emotional help you need.)

Are you hiding a sin you need to share? If you are experiencing conviction, ask the Lord to give you the boldness to do what's needed. Know that repentance is the path to forgiveness.

A Prayer Against Shame

LORD, BATHSHEBA'S GOD ENCOUNTER
reminds me that my shameful circumstances
are yours to redeem. Whether what happened was
by my own doing, like David, or was done to me, like
Bathsheba, you offer redemption. If I committed sins
I've kept hidden, I can echo the words David wrote
when he sinned against Bathsheba: "Create in me a
clean heart, O God, and renew a right spirit within
me" (Ps. 51:10). If, like Bathsheba, I've been a victim
of abuse, I can know that you are near to the brokenhearted and save those who are crushed in spirit
(Ps. 34:18). Help me know, not just intellectually, but in
every part of my being, that I'm a loved daughter
of God. Help me believe that you will bind my wounds
and that even if justice cannot be had on earth,
you will provide justice ultimately and eternally.

The Widow of Zarephath
A Faith that Lives

She is gathering sticks for a fire. The land is dry and barren in her Phoenician seaport village of Zarephath. There has been a severe drought: all living things have dried up, and soon she and her only son will dry up and return to the earth themselves. All she has left is a little flour and some oil. There is nothing to do but make one last meal and wait for death.

"Can you bring me a little water in a vessel that I might drink?" a voice says behind her.

She looks up, her eyes meeting those of a stranger. Somehow, she knows that he is a holy man. And she is right—he is Elijah, the prophet of Israel.

His God is not her god. She is a Baal worshiper. She owes him nothing. But she does have some water she can offer this dusty, weary traveler.

"And might I have a morsel of bread too?"

Now this was too much.

"I don't have any bread," says the woman, exasperation creeping into her voice. "I only have a handful of flour in a jar and some olive oil in a jug. I was just gathering these sticks to take home and make a meal for myself and my son, so that we could eat it—and die."

Then the woman—known in Scripture only as a widow—receives a response she doesn't anticipate.

"Don't be afraid. Go and do as you have said," Elijah instructs. "But first make me a small cake of bread and bring it to me, and afterward make something for yourself and your son. For this is what the Lord God of Israel says, 'The jar of flour shall not become empty, and the jug of oil shall not run dry, until the day that the Lord sends rain upon the land.'"

For some reason, the widow decides to take a chance. Maybe she figures she has nothing to lose? She has nothing to look forward to but death. But maybe what this prophet says will come true. It is just a small glimmer of hope. Little does she know she is doing exactly what the God of Israel had planned for her to do (1 Kings 17:9).

And so, with just a tiny bit of faith, the widow's hands reach for the flour and then the oil. Every time she reaches for it, there is just enough for one more cake of bread. Just like the Israelites' faith was tested each day as they relied on their daily manna, the widow's faith is tested every time she dips her hand into the flour or pours out the oil. There is never an abundance. There is just enough for that day.

And so she lives. So does her son. When drought, death, and destruction are all around them, the widow and her household stay alive. God had purposely brought on the drought due to Israel's sin, and others outside of Israel were experiencing these consequences as well. Elijah told Israel's king at the time, the evil King Ahab, whom the Bible says did more evil than all the leaders who came before him, to expect no rain or even dew. While God's own people are far from him, this foreign woman receives faith and mercy.

But then, when the danger of starvation seems past, illness strikes her son. Life leaves his body. That which she had been trying to avoid comes true, despite the miracle of flour and oil.

The widow is confused and in despair. They have survived drought and starvation, yet her son is still marked to die? This is worse than if they'd simply died together in famine! Now all that is precious to her is gone. She has survived, but what is the point of living without her son? Her faith grew with each new day of provision, but now it is struck down, withering like the grass all around them.

"What do you have against me?" the widow lashes out against Elijah in her anger and grief. "You've come only to remind me of my sin and kill my son!"

Elijah pleads with God on behalf of the widow for her son's life. He takes the child's lifeless form and carries him upstairs to where he has been staying and privately begs God to intervene on behalf of the widow's son. "Lord, why have you brought tragedy to this widow by killing her son?" he questions. Elijah stretches himself out over the boy three times, praying all the while that the Lord would give the boy's life back to him. God listens to Elijah and grants his request, breathing life back into the limp body of the boy.

"Look, your son is alive," Elijah exclaims, presenting the now living and breathing boy to his mother.

"Now I know that you are a man of God, and that the word of the Lord is true," the widow tells Elijah with incredible gratitude. Just as the son is brought to life again, so is the widow's faith. Her encounter with God raising her son demolishes whatever doubts she still harbored in her heart.

A GENTILE RECEIVES FAITH

Why did God care about this unnamed widow? Why did he solidify her faith by raising her son to life? Was it simply because Elijah asked? Was it because the woman had already exhibited faith by feeding God's prophet instead of keeping her food for herself and her son? Did God want to strip her of any remaining doubt that he was, indeed, the true God?

We don't know. What we *do* know is that God cared for this Gentile woman who had very little to give, and he rewarded her for her faith and her quivering act of obedience and hospitality. She obeyed God when it seemed futile, when it seemed like nothing but darkness and death awaited. Instead of death she was given life, life everlasting. Perhaps, since God's own people had forsaken him to follow other gods, he decided to lavish his grace on someone else instead.

In the New Testament we're given a clue as to why. Jesus himself mentions this woman, early in his ministry. In Luke 4 he is in his own hometown of Nazareth. After reading from the book of Isaiah where he prophesied the coming Messiah, Jesus tells the crowd he has fulfilled this Scripture. The congregation is shocked, and begins murmuring, "Isn't this Joseph's son?" Basically they're saying, "Isn't this the guy we grew up with, he's no one special!"

In response to his hometown questioning his divinity, Jesus brings up the widow of Zarephath:

Truly I tell you, no prophet is accepted in his hometown. But I say to you, there were certainly many widows in Israel in Elijah's days, when the sky was shut up for three years and six months while a great famine came over all the land. Yet Elijah was not sent to any of them except a widow at Zarephath in Sidon. And in the prophet Elisha's time, there were many in Israel who had leprosy, and yet not one of them was cleansed except Naaman the Syrian. (Luke 4:24–27 CSB)

At this pronouncement of judgment for unbelief, the congregation turns into a murderous mob and attempts to kill Jesus, but he escapes. Jesus seems to be suggesting that when his people reject their own prophets, the prophets will go to outsiders, even Gentiles. When the gift of faith is accepted, Jesus will lavish his grace and salvation on that person, no matter who they are.

I want to follow the widow of Zarephath's example. Even when no trace of hope is seen, I too, want to take a shaky step of faith and obey God's word. The first step of faith is the step of salvation. When we receive Jesus as our Savior we are taking the first step of obedience in faith. The second step is simply continued obedience to what his word reveals to us in the Bible and letting that word change us to be more like Christ. That step is called sanctification. Sanctification is a continual and life-long process as we grow in faith and obedience and learn how to live out a Christ-filled life.

THE WIDOW OF ZAREPHATH'S
GOD ENCOUNTER:

One of the most striking examples of faith comes not from the more famous women of the Bible but from an unnamed foreign widow. In a quivering act of obedience, this woman puts her faith in God. And so can we.

GETTING TO THE HEART

Read 1 Kings 17:8–24.

Have you accepted Christ as your Savior? This is the first step of faith and obedience every person must take.

If you are already a Christian, is there an area in your life you need to step out in obedience to God? Your obedience may seem as small as the widow of Zarephath's flour and oil, but God can multiply all things. Does your obedience seem futile or even frightening? How can you take the first step?

Is there some suffering that you've experienced that's strengthened your faith? Reflect on how you've grown stronger through suffering.

A Prayer for Obedience

LORD, SOMETIMES OBEDIENCE
seems scary or even useless. Help me seek to
obey you no matter what the cost. Even in the midst of
suffering, help me choose obedience. No matter what
I lack, help me choose generosity. No matter the
drought, help me have faith for hope to rain again.

The Shunammite Woman

A GENEROUS MIRACLE

She holds her dead son in her arms.

A wave of grief washes over her as she cradles his still-warm body against her chest. She doesn't know how long she sits there, in a daze of disbelief. He had just been playing in the fields while her husband oversaw the harvest, and now he is motionless and silent. He had complained of pain in his head, so a servant had carried him in from the fields and laid him on her lap, and she had held him in her arms until he died. Now she tenderly lifts him and takes him upstairs to the room she had built for Elisha, the prophet of God. Once inside the room, she lays her son on the bed, arranging his still form with care. Then, shutting the door behind her, she swiftly goes in search of her husband.

"I need you to send me a servant with one of the donkeys, so that I can quickly find Elisha and come back again," she says to her husband.

"Why do you need to go today?" asks her husband. "It is not a new moon or a Sabbath day."

"All is well," she assures him, "but I must see him." Saddling the donkey, she urges both the animal and the servant who accompanies her to hurry, determined not to stop for anything until she finds Elisha at Mount Carmel.

HOSPITALITY IN ACTION

Elisha, a prophet of God, often passed through Shunem, and after a while the woman urged him to stop and eat in her home. As time passed and she got to know him more, she even built a room for the prophet on the roof of her house, complete with a bed, table, chair, and lamp so he could be comfortable when he was in their region.

A wealthy woman, she was happy to be able to use her finances to bless this man who seemed to have few earthly possessions apart from what he carried with him. She was pleased to see him use the items she'd picked out for his comfort.

Time passed, and then there was that pivotal and slightly awkward conversation. Elisha's servant, Gehazi, had asked her if there was anything they could do for her, such as speak on her behalf to the king or the commander of the army. She'd assured them that she had all she needed; living among her own people, with her wealth, she lacked nothing. She wanted to make sure he knew there was no need to pay back her generosity. But later, Gehazi had called her up to Elisha's room. She stood in the doorway feeling a little awkward even in her own house.

Then the man had said something so stunning she'd been shocked and almost hurt.

"Around this time next year you shall hold a son," Elisha had declared matter-of-factly.

She felt suddenly like someone had looked deep inside her soul and spoke into her most closely held desire and bitterest disappointment. Hope flared up inside her and she quickly tried to tamp it down with common sense. What was this man playing at, declaring such a thing that he knew nothing about?

"Oh no, my lord, O man of God; do not lie to your servant," she'd whispered, almost begging Elisha. She had learned to control this longing deep inside her and had no desire to bring it to the surface of her emotions again. She had long since stopped dreaming such a thing could happen to her.

Elisha had said no more about it, and she felt like she had been dismissed. But almost a year later she had, to her amazement, held the longed-for son in her arms.

Before having her son, she'd learned to be content. Her life had been good. But after her son was born, she experienced more joy than she'd known was possible. And now, all that joy had been ripped away. She had been fine, *fine*, before a son had been born. And now she'd never be fine again.

She urges the donkey to go faster.

ALL IS NOT WELL

Gehazi comes down the mountain path to greet her.

"Is all well with you? Is all well with your husband? Is all well with the child?" he calls to her as he swiftly moves toward her.

"All is well," she says simply. She doesn't even slow down; Elisha's servant is not who she's come to see. She's come to see Elisha.

Gehazi turns to follow her as she continues up the mountain path until she reaches Elisha. She slides off the donkey and onto the ground, gripping Elisha's feet, unable to speak.

Gehazi reaches down to pull her away from Elisha, but Elisha intervenes.

"Can't you see she's in bitter distress?" Elisha says to Gehazi. "The Lord has hidden it from me and not told me what it is."

She lifts tear-filled eyes to Elisha's wrinkled-worn ones.

"Did I ask my lord for a son? Did I not say, 'Do not deceive me?'" Her voice is full of sorrow and her implied accusation hangs in the air.

Then Elisha turns to Gehazi. "Tie up your garment and run! Lay my staff on the face of the child. Don't stop to talk to anyone on the way."

But the woman grips him even more firmly and says, "As the Lord lives and as you yourself live, I will not leave you." She is not going to be satisfied with Gehazi, a mere servant. Only Elisha himself will do.

Elisha and the woman set out towards Shunem, with Gehazi going on ahead at a faster pace. When he arrives at her home, he does exactly what Elisha said, but nothing happens.

When Elisha arrives, he climbs up to the little room to find the child lying on his bed waiting for him. He shuts the door behind him.

The woman paces downstairs, listening, praying, hoping—barely breathing. All is quiet upstairs. She waits in tense silence, every muscle taut as her whole body strains, listening. She dares not even speak what she seeks, what she hopes for, even to herself.

Then there are seven sneezes. She counts them. One. Two. Three. Four. Five. Six. Seven.

Gehazi calls down to her. She rushes up onto the roof of the house and through the door of the room she'd built for this mysterious man of God.

Elisha is sitting on the bed with her son in his lap . . . *alive*.

"Pick up your son," he says, eyes crinkling like laughter at the corners.

Her knees buckle and she falls at his feet. This time she doesn't grab them in grief, but she weeps with relief. And holy amazement.

Then she picks up her son and leaves the room.

ALL IS WELL

The Shunammite woman experienced something that few people have experienced in this life: an earthly resurrection. Thus far in our look at these biblical mothers, only a poor widow and a wealthy woman received back their dead children, one by Elijah and the other by Elisha, both a conduit of God's power.

The Shunammite woman's generosity set the stage for this miracle. Because of her lavish attention to the needs of Elisha, he in turn was generous to her. She saw what he lacked, and she provided it. He saw what *she* lacked and asked God to provide it. Her blessing to Elisha birthed a blessing back to her.

Then tragedy struck. Her blessing was taken away.

Oddly, the Shunammite woman was questioned by both her husband and Elisha's servant and her response to both men was *all is well*. Of course, all was *not* well. Her response was almost laughable. Who says such a thing in the face of their only child's death? In an amazing display of self-control, she doesn't explain to them what happened. It doesn't seem like she told her husband their son has even died, although one would assume he knew since the child wasn't feeling well. In an amazing act of faith, she saddled her donkey and without letting anyone get in her way, made a beeline for Elisha, who was approximately twenty miles away depending on what route she may have taken while riding a donkey. She'd have spent the whole afternoon making the journey and probably reached Mount Carmel by early evening, depending on how fast she was able to travel.

Despite the fact that she had declared "all is well," Elisha saw through her assurance and knew that all was wrong. Elisha sent his servant to do the job of resurrecting her son, but she wouldn't accept a substitute for Elisha. She wanted the man himself. She hadn't traveled for hours for a substitute for the man of God. So, she and Elisha began the journey back to her home at a slower pace, possibly not arriving back at her home until the next day.

The Shunammite woman believed something could be done for her. The prophet had declared her child would be born before she had even conceived. Was it so crazy to think he could do something about her son's death? The Shunammite woman seemed to think so and spoke a prophecy into her own life: *all is well.* She wouldn't leave until God showed up on behalf of her child.

Her hope in the face of adversity reminds me of the poem *Four Quartets* by T.S. Eliot. In it he echoes words attributed to Julian of Norwich:

And all shall be well and
All manner of thing shall be well
When the tongues of flames are in-folded
Into the crowned knot of fire
And the fire and the rose are one.[12]

This poem captures the tension in the Shunammite woman's story. All was not well, but she declared that it was. She speaks life and hope into her situation despite the "knot of fire" of death she is experiencing. She doesn't know how things are going to work out. She doesn't know if her son will be returned to her. But she decides to find the one person in her life who has access to the power of God and beseech him for a miracle with every fiber of her being, level with the ground, grabbing his feet.

DIRECT ACCESS

Unlike the Shunammite woman, we don't need to saddle a donkey, get in our car, or even find a "man of God." We can go directly to the power source. Hebrews 4:16 reminds us that we have the confidence to "draw near to the throne of grace, that we may receive mercy and find grace to help in time of need." The Shunammite woman shows us what to do in our time of need: run to the throne of grace. We can rest in God's sovereignty knowing *all is well* even while we are simultaneously praying for him to change our circumstances. We can whisper *all is well,* knowing we are being held in the palm of his hand while we beg him to lift us from the metaphorical pit. In our time of need, God is there with us. The two do not conflict. We can fall at his feet and ask him to show up in our lives and give us a miracle. We don't need a go-between; Christ has already come. We can pray, we can make our requests known to God, and we can wait to see what he will do, knowing that whether we get our miracle or not, *all is well.* We are loved, we are held in his everlasting arms, and he won't let us go.

THE SHUNAMMITE WOMAN'S GOD ENCOUNTER:

This unnamed woman used her wealth to provide hospitality to a prophet of God and is blessed for doing so. Her act of generosity results in a stunning miracle and an encounter with God like few people have ever experienced. She trusts in God, declaring *all is well* even when she doesn't know how her story will end.

GETTING TO THE HEART

Read 2 Kings 4:8–37.

Is there an area in your life where God is asking you to give generously? Is there a need you see that you can fulfill?

Are you in need of God supernaturally showing up in your life? Does it feel silly or even like you aren't trusting God to beg him to show up in your life or the life of another in a way that seems ridiculously impossible?

A Prayer for a Miracle

LORD, IN THESE DAYS OF SCIENCE AND REASON
it can feel stupid to ask for a miracle. It might even
feel like I'm not trusting your sovereignty to ask for my
circumstances to change. But with the author
of Lamentations I can cry, "I called on Your name,
O Lord, out of the lowest pit. You have heard my voice,
'Do not hide Your ear from my prayer for relief,
From my cry for help.' You drew near when I called on
You; You said, 'Do not fear!'" (Lam. 3:55–57 NASB).
You are willing to hear my heart's cry and I'm willing
to trust you with the outcome, to say *all is well*
even while kneeling before you to ask you
to intervene on my behalf.

Elizabeth

FAITH FOR THE BARREN YEARS

Elizabeth is going about her daily tasks when she hears a voice behind her call out a greeting. At that moment, her unborn baby boy makes a sudden movement that almost takes her breath away. Elizabeth is filled with the Holy Spirit as she turns around and sees her kinswoman Mary unexpectedly at her door.

"Blessed are you among women," she loudly exclaims, instantaneously having insight into the reason Mary is there to visit her—insight that can only be explained by the Holy Spirit's revelation to her. Now she knows who the baby growing in her womb will be making a way for. "Blessed is the fruit of your womb! Why should the mother of my Lord come see me? When I heard your greeting, the baby in my womb leaped for joy. Blessed is she who believed that there would be a fulfillment of what was spoken to her from the Lord."

The two women hug each other, joyful both because they are together again and because each woman holds a miraculously promised child in her womb.

A DAUGHTER OF AARON

Elizabeth kept the letter of the law, and not only in the outward sense: she was righteous before God. For years she had lived a life that was blameless before the Lord. She was not perfect, of course, but Scripture didn't record a single word of reproach about her life. Instead Scripture praised her, saying she and her husband were "both righteous before God, walking blamelessly in all the commandments and statutes of the Lord" (Luke 1:6).

Still, she was barren. And like the women before her—Sarah, Rachel, and Hannah—she viewed it as a disgrace. And so did everyone else.

She was a descendant of Aaron. She was married to a priest. Why would God not bless her with a child? What had she done? Why were her prayers going unanswered? And now, like Sarah, she was old.

Yet Elizabeth was faithful. Her life was saturated with a vital and personal love for God.

Can you imagine the wonder she must have felt when Zechariah returned home from serving the Lord in the temple—mute no less—writing on a tablet that an angel had visited him, and they would have a son? Don't you wish her response was recorded for us?

Zechariah had the unique privilege of being chosen by God to burn incense in the temple. Incense would have been burned each morning and evening, a multi-sensory representation of the prayers of the people who were praying outside. During this special moment, however, Zechariah was startled by the appearance of the angel Gabriel, who told Zechariah that his wife would finally have a son, and not just any son. A son named John who would be given the mission of turning many hearts of the people of Israel back towards the Lord. He would have the spirit and power of Elijah! Although the angel told him not to be frightened and said that he was there to answer Zechariah's prayers, Zechariah remained unconvinced and doubted the entire situation. In return, Gabriel made Zechariah unable to speak and told him he wouldn't have his voice back until his prophecy came true.

Elizabeth was soon with child, just as Gabriel predicted. Interestingly, Elizabeth chose to hide herself away for five months after she conceived. This was not a cultural necessity but a personal choice. It seemed that she wanted to keep the news of her pregnancy a secret for a while. Perhaps her joy was so profound she wanted to savor it. Perhaps she wanted to prepare herself for the new work the Lord was going to have her do as she raised a special son. But one thing was certain. She worshiped the Lord when she proclaimed, "The Lord has done this for me. He has looked with favor in these days to take away my disgrace among the people" (Luke 1:25 CSB). Elizabeth's words closely echoed those of Rachel who, when she finally gave birth after years of barrenness, also said, "God has taken away my disgrace" (Gen. 30:23). Like Rachel before her, she was thankful the Lord had remembered her.

A SPECIAL VISITOR

It was in Elizabeth's sixth month of pregnancy that her relative, Mary, got her own news of a supernatural pregnancy. During this announcement the angel of the Lord informed Mary that Elizabeth too had conceived, despite her advancing age. Mary quickly left to go visit Elizabeth, and what a blessing it was that these two godly women had each other to confide in.

Elizabeth acknowledged with faith the Lord's work in both their lives, and the two women worshiped the Lord. What talks they must have had! They could speak with all earnestness without fear of ridicule or judgment, knowing that they were sharing a common experience that no one else understood.

The Bible says that Mary stayed with Elizabeth for three months. Since six plus three make nine, Mary was probably present for John's birth. She might have even stayed for his circumcision and witnessed the return of Zechariah's voice.

At last, the long-awaited son was placed in Elizabeth's weathered arms. Tiny and wrinkled, swaddled in a blanket, Elizabeth held her miracle—a miracle not just meant for her, but the nation of Israel. God had it all planned from the beginning.

Eight days after her baby's birth, Elizabeth's strong faith was once again revealed at her son's circumcision: as those around her tried to name her son after his father, as was the custom, Elizabeth intervened.

"No; he shall be called John," Elizabeth responded simply and resolutely. This was the name Gabriel had told Zechariah to name him.

Those gathered appealed to her husband, but Zechariah responded by agreeing with Elizabeth. Immediately, his speech returned!

All the visiting relatives and neighbors were overcome with a holy fear. Something strange was going on. The news spread all through the hill country of Judea. Everyone was talking, and this time it was not to judge Elizabeth's barrenness, but to exclaim over the mysterious circumstances of the birth of her son. Something special and strange was happening and everyone took notice.

And what of Elizabeth? I think we can assume she raised her child as faithfully as she had lived out her years of barrenness. That she taught her son, John the Baptist, to live righteous and blameless before the Lord.

Did she live to see him full-grown, a locust-eating prophet living and teaching in the wilderness? Did she know he baptized his cousin, Jesus? Did she hear of his imprisonment and beheading?

We don't know. But however long Elizabeth lived, I think she continued to live a life of faith. She'd been faithful through the long barren years; how could she not continue faithfully after all she'd seen and experienced?

BARREN PLACES

Barrenness may take many forms in life. We all have barren places that are seemingly a wasteland. A longed-for dream that is good and godly just won't come true. Our health or the health of a loved one senselessly snatched away. A once vibrant relationship now riddled with dissention. We may interpret barren places as judgment or punishment from God and wonder why he would inflict such pain on us—did we do something wrong? Sometimes barrenness may be a consequence of sinful living. However, God's sovereign plan is always at work, and in Elizabeth's case, he had something special in mind. Her greatest reproach or disgrace had nothing to do with anything she'd done. Not at all. In the end God not only filled her empty womb with a child, he also even filled her with his Holy Spirit.

Elisabeth Elliot encourages us in her book *Secure in the Everlasting Arms* with this thought:

> In the barren places of my life I can be assured that God is there as He is when life is fruitful, and that the time is coming (give me patience, Lord, to wait!) when He will fulfill His word: "I will put in the desert the cedar and the acacia, the myrtle and the olive. I will set pines in the wasteland, the fir and the cypress together, so that people may see and know, may consider and understand, that the hand of the Lord has done this" (Isaiah 41:19-20).[13]

So, the question becomes, will I continue in faithfulness, despite the lack I currently see?

ELIZABETH'S GOD'S ENCOUNTER:

The Bible says Elizabeth and her husband were a righteous and blameless couple. But Elizabeth may have wondered why God allowed her to be barren, since culturally it was viewed as a disgrace. Still, Elizabeth didn't grow bitter towards God. Instead, she beautifully demonstrated what it means to be faithful in the barren years—even when life didn't go as planned.

GETTING TO THE HEART

Read Luke 1.

Barrenness can take many forms. How have you experienced "barrenness" in your own life?

Elizabeth shows us how to live through disappointment. How can Elizabeth's example of faithfulness during dry times encourage you in your own daily life?

Will you continue in righteousness despite an unanswered prayer in your life or the life of your child? Will you continue to be a faithful worshiper even if you experience the disappointment of not conceiving a child? Experience illness? The death of a child?

A Prayer During Barrenness

LORD, CIRCUMSTANCES AREN'T GREAT RIGHT NOW.
I've tried to follow you, obey you, love you, and seek
your will but sometimes it seems like I'm being
punished. Sometimes Christian culture preaches
"if you do these things . . . God will bless you," but we
know that's not always the way it goes because of all
the stories we see in the Bible that prove this thinking
wrong. In Scripture, the people who follow you
suffer often, and we don't always know exactly why.
Job even suffered *because* he was so righteous!
Help me follow Elizabeth's example and be a woman of
faith in the barren years. Help me look for the comfort
of your presence no matter the difficult
circumstance or unrealized dream.

Mary

A HUMBLE HEART

It is a quiet morning. Mary is home alone and sitting in a sunny corner of the room mending her clothes. She is happy and content, thinking about her future. She is engaged to a good man named Joseph, who makes his living as a carpenter. Her future seems secure and promising.

Suddenly, feeling a presence in the room, she looks up and there stands a strange man, shining unlike anything she's ever seen.

"Greetings, the Lord is with you," says the man—the angel, Gabriel. The very same one who also brought Zechariah his message.

Mary doesn't respond at first because she is troubled and unsure about what is happening. The angel continues, "Do not be afraid, Mary, for you have found favor with God. Now listen: You will conceive and give birth to a son, and you will name him Jesus. He will be great and will be called the Son of the Most High, and the Lord God will give him the throne of his father David. He will reign over the house of Jacob forever, and his kingdom will have no end" (Luke 1:30–33 CSB).

"I am a virgin, so how will this happen?" Mary asks in wonder.

"The Holy Spirit will come upon you and the power of the Most High will overshadow you," the angel explains. "The child born to you will be holy and called the Son of God. Also, your relative Elizabeth has conceived a son in her old age, and she is six months pregnant. Nothing is impossible with God."

"I am the Lord's servant," said Mary. "May it happen to me as you have said."

The angel leaves her.

Mary sits in stunned silence, trying to comprehend what has just happened.

AN INCONVENIENT PREGNANCY

Inconvenient.

If ever there was an inconvenient pregnancy, it was Mary's. Her pregnancy was not only miraculous; it put her in a tenuous situation. As a virgin engaged to be married Mary could have been stoned to death for adultery (Deut. 22:23–24). Engagements during biblical times were more binding than those today. They were a legal agreement that was only breakable by divorce.

There's so much I wonder about. I would love to know the details of what Mary went through. What did Mary's parents say? When she went away to visit Elizabeth for three months and came back showing signs of pregnancy, how did she deal with the gossip? Did she remain silent, or did she share the angel's message? Was she laughed at and ridiculed? Did people assume the father was Joseph?

There's no evidence that she worried over her reputation—although we know from Joseph's response that he did not believe her at first (Matt. 1:20–21). However, being a man of character, he decided he would divorce her quietly instead of demanding capital punishment. Instead of worrying about Joseph, her parents, or the neighbors, Mary revealed herself to be mature in her faith when receiving this unbelievable news. She joyfully accepted this surprising mission for her life with humble reverence.

Although I wish I knew the details, what I *do* know is that Mary did not bring up these potential challenges and fears to the angel Gabriel who visited her on that miraculous day. However, these concerns must have certainly crashed into her mind the minute the angel left. She only had one question, and it was a good one. How could she get pregnant when she'd never even been with a man? That was the question she wanted answered.

After receiving Gabriel's answer, she responded with incredible humility:

"I am the Lord's servant. May it happen to me as you have said."

How I long to respond to the inconveniences in my life like Mary. *I am the Lord's servant. May it happen to me as you have said.*

Motherhood is *all* about inconvenience. The physical discomfort of a swelling body is just the beginning. Next comes the intensity of labor. Then the late-night feedings, poopy diapers, and perhaps, inconsolable crying? The reality begins to hit that one's life really isn't one's own anymore. Of course, joy is experienced in every one of those situations, but sometimes, motherhood is just plain inconvenient.

Even the smallest inconveniences can sometimes send me for a tailspin. Perhaps I'm interrupted when a child wakes up early from a nap when I'm trying to do something "spiritual" like study my Bible. Perhaps I'm staying up late to have me-time and catch up on my favorite show when a child gets sick. My natural tendency is to not be happy when I'm interrupted. This is *my* time, after all. Whoever is interrupting me—usually the kids—are invading it. They're, well, inconvenient. My mother's heart does not naturally desire to sacrifice for them. I don't want to give up the time that I thought was allotted to me. While I'd gladly die for my kids, sometimes it's the smaller sacrifices that are the hardest for me. C.S. Lewis noted this tension and made this startling observation:

> The great thing, if one can, is to stop regarding all the unpleasant things as interruptions of one's "own," or "real" life. The truth is of course that what one calls the interruptions are precisely one's real life—the life God is sending one day by day: what one calls one's "real life" is a phantom of one's own imagination. This at least is what I see at moments of insight: but it's hard to remember it all the time.[14]

Lewis is right, it *is* hard to remember all the time. But what if the interruptions I face aren't interruptions at all? What if they are actually God's plan for my day?

For Mary, the high honor of being the mother of Jesus came with interruptions and inconveniences that would culminate in great suffering. She suffered by giving birth in a stable, by fleeing to Egypt while toddlers were slain by order of royal edict, because King Herod was looking for *her* son (can you imagine living with that knowledge?). She suffered when Jesus left his family after thirty years to accomplish his earthly ministry and she did not have access to him as she did before (Mark 3:31–35). She experienced the pain of family turmoil because her *other* sons didn't believe Jesus was the Christ (John 7:5). Finally, she suffered the ultimate pain of seeing her son crucified. Indeed, the sword pierced her side, just as Simeon prophesied when she took baby Jesus to the temple to be dedicated (Luke 2:25–35).

Despite all her pain, Mary remained humble, not proud and demanding, even though she knew she'd be remembered through the ages as Jesus' mother. She was aware the story wasn't really about her in the first place. It was about *him*. And nowhere is this more evident than in the fact that Mary herself was a disciple of Christ. You might even say she was his first disciple. If anyone knew the truth about Jesus, it was Mary. She knew beyond a shadow of a doubt the supernatural way he was conceived. When she met with Elizabeth for the first time and the women bonded over their shared experience of miraculous conceptions, Mary became his first worshiper when she proclaimed:

> My soul magnifies the Lord,
> and my spirit rejoices in God my Savior,
> because he has looked with favor
> on the humble condition of his servant.
> Surely, from now on all generations
> will call me blessed,
> because the Mighty One
> has done great things for me,
> and his name is holy.

His mercy is from generation to generation
on those who fear him.
He has done a mighty deed with his arm;
he has scattered the proud
because of the thoughts of their hearts;
he has toppled the mighty from their thrones
and exalted the lowly.
He has satisfied the hungry with good things
and sent the rich away empty.
He has helped his servant Israel,
remembering his mercy
to Abraham and his descendants forever,
just as he spoke to our ancestors. (Luke 1:46–55 CSB)

Mary's hymn of praise was one of complete humility, wonder, joy, and confidence in God her Savior. And for the rest of her life, she'd treasure and ponder these wonders in her heart (Luke 2:19, 51).

Gien Karssen summarized Mary's life beautifully when she wrote that Mary experienced "unknown pinnacles of happiness. At the same time she had experienced deep heart sorrows, which no other woman has or ever will encounter. But her attitude toward God hadn't changed. She had proven with her life that she meant the words she spoke when the Messiah was announced, 'I am the Lord's servant, and I will do whatever He desires.'"[15] Through it all, Mary was there. She was a witness to it all. The last time we see Mary in Scripture, Jesus has risen and ascended. We find her in Jerusalem, gathered with the eleven disciples and the other women who were Jesus' followers. She was not left alone. Not only that, but her other sons were also now with her. In the end, they too chose to believe. And that is our last sighting of Mary, the mother of Jesus, a disciple of her own Son and devoted in prayer with other believers.

I pray Mary's humble response to the Lord's will for her life would be my response too—not only in motherhood, but in all of life.

MARY'S GOD ENCOUNTER:

Mary demonstrated great humility, aware that her story wasn't really about her in the first place. It was about Jesus. And Mary herself was a disciple of Christ and she uniquely showed what it meant to be a follower of Jesus.

GETTING TO THE HEART

Read Luke 1–2.

Where is God calling you to submit with humility to His plans for your life? Do you consider it an inconvenience or a blessing?

Do you view life's interruptions as an opportunity for divine conversations and interactions instead of just a hassle to be gotten through?

A Prayer for Humility

LORD, IN THIS CULTURE HUMILITY
seems like weakness. A humble heart isn't
admired. If anything, pride is championed and
held up as an example to follow. Doing humble jobs
can feel embarrassing—even jobs we intellectually
know are important, like motherhood. Help me not
worry about what others think of me. No doubt many
considered Mary a fornicator, but Lord, you knew the
type of woman she really was and blessed her.
It was by accepting your blessing that she received
judgment from her neighbors. Help me be humble
about what you bring into my life as well—
and help me not focus on what others think.

Salome

MISPLACED AMBITION

She comes before him, kneeling. Her sons, James and John, stand beside her. They are two of Jesus of Nazareth's closest disciples and have given up working in the family fishing business to follow him (Matt. 4:21–22). Jesus himself has nicknamed them the "Sons of Thunder," which makes her smile (Mark 3:16–17). Her mind goes back over the story they've told her about how they witnessed Jesus transform before their very eyes, shining white as light, while speaking to Moses and Elijah. They have seen too much not to believe—Jesus has to be the Messiah!

Now, a question burns within her. And he sees it.

"What do you want?" Jesus asks her.

"I would like you to promise me that one day my two sons will sit in your kingdom, one at your right hand and one at your left," she says.

"You do not know what you are asking," Jesus tells her. Then he turns his eyes to the Sons of Thunder. "Are you able to drink the cup that I am about to drink?"

"We are able," they reply confidently.

"You will drink my cup, but to sit at my right or my left is not my decision to make. It is for my Father to decide who will sit there."

That is it—the conversation is over. Salome fades back into the crowd that always hangs around Jesus while the other ten disciples begin to argue with James and John, affronted they've put themselves forward in such a bold way. There are accusations and arguments put forth as to why other disciples should be given the honor to be seated on Jesus' right and left hand.

Finally, Jesus' voice cuts through the bickering: "Gentile rulers brag about their authority, but it should not be that way with you. If you want to be great, you must be a servant. Whoever wants to be first among you must be a slave. The Son of Man came not to *be* served but *to* serve and give his life as a ransom for many."

Salome is puzzled over this saying. This is the third time that Jesus has said *the first will be last and the last will be first.* It is obviously significant. First, he had said it at the end of a story about vineyard laborers and how they'd all received a denarius at the end of their workday—no matter when they had started. Those who worked from morning until evening received a denarius and so did the workers who had only worked an hour! Then, he had used the phrase after a rich young man had asked him about gaining eternal life. Jesus said it would be easier for a camel to go through the eye of a needle than a rich person to enter the kingdom of God. Then he had said, "But many who are first will be last, and the last first." Unlike the rich young man, her boys had thrown away everything to follow Jesus. They had given up their fishing business with their father. Certainly, they deserved to be sitting on the throne with Jesus!

The first will be last and the last will be first.
What did it mean?

. . .

Salome stands huddled with Mary Magdalene and the other women who follow Jesus. She is numb with grief and shock. The earth shakes while darkness rolls in, frightening them all.

Jesus cries out, "My God, my God, why have you forsaken me?"

Some people nearby say he is calling Elijah. Even a Roman centurion who is overseeing the execution has been visibly disturbed.

And then, Jesus draws his last breath.

It isn't supposed to be this way; this is not what she's been expecting. That's when she remembers what Jesus said when she had asked for her sons to sit on his right and left hand when he came into his kingdom: "But whoever would be great among you must be your servant, and however would be first among you must be your slave, even as the Son of Man came not to be served but to serve, and to give his life as a ransom for many" (Matt. 20:26–28).

Where was his kingdom now? What did it mean?

. . .

Three days later they walk silently, each entangled in her own thoughts, each grieving in her own way: Mary Magdalene, Mary (who also had a son named James who was a disciple), and Salome. They are on a common mission; they carry spices with them and plan to prepare Jesus' body for a final proper burial. They had been rushed and delayed by the coming Sabbath when Jesus had died, now they hurry to Jesus' resting place to complete the embalming. The two Marys knew the way because they had seen him buried in Joseph of Arimathea's tomb.

The sun is just rising, sending warm rays across the landscape, driving back the shadows of the night.

"What will we do when we get there?" Mary Magdalene wonders out loud. "We aren't strong enough to roll the stone from the entrance."

They hadn't wanted to bother the men. Everyone was so worn out from the events of the past few days. But as they come around a bend in the garden path, they see Joseph of Arimathea's tomb, and the stone has already been rolled from the entrance.

They all pause and look at each other, hesitant and questioning. Silently, they enter the dark cavern cut from rock.

Then they gasp in awe! There is a young man sitting off to the right, radiant in a white robe.

"Do not be alarmed," he says calmly. "You are looking for Jesus of Nazareth, who was crucified. He is risen; he is not here. See the place where they laid him. He's gone. Go tell his disciples that he is going before you to Galilee. There you will see him, just like he told you he would."

They back out of the tomb in astonishment, practically tripping over each other, spices dropping to the ground. Then they run, trembling in hope and fear.

As she runs, Salome's feet pound out the question, what did it mean?

KINGDOM-FOCUSED AMBITION

Salome was the mother of James and John, two of Jesus' disciples, and she may have even been the sister of Mary, the mother of Jesus, because John 19:25 says that "standing by the cross of Jesus were his mother and his mother's sister." In the two other passages that describe this same scene, Salome was specifically noted as being at the cross, while in this passage the same group of women were mentioned by name except for the person noted to be Mary's sister, which may be a reference to Salome. If this is so, that means James and John were actually Jesus' cousins. Of course, it could be referring to another woman as well, because Matthew said there were "many" women at the cross. Regardless, Salome also was a follower of Jesus, along with her more famous sons.

Salome made a request of Jesus to grant her sons special status in his kingdom, which she probably imagined—like many others—would be fulfilled on earth. The same story is also told in Mark 10:35–45 but it doesn't include Salome; it's framed only as a request by James and John. This could indicate it was their idea to make this request and that she was simply speaking for them, or that passage just didn't include her as part of the conversation. Whether she was asking on the behalf of her sons or whether it was her own idea, the request reveals both her heart and the heart of her sons. Salome seemed to recognize Jesus as the Messiah and acknowledged he will be ushering in a kingdom.

However, this request revealed her misplaced ambition for her sons. She was still viewing status from a worldly framework, not a kingdom framework. The irony of her request was that she asked directly after Jesus revealed to his followers that he would be mocked, flogged, and crucified and then raised on the third day. In the midst of this declaration, Salome approached and asked that her sons be elevated over all the other disciples to sit at Jesus' right and left, a place of honor and distinction. She completely missed the point.

The lesson Jesus had been trying to make stick in his disciples' heads was that the first will be last and the last will be first. Her request flew in the face of this ideal. He had repeated some version of this lesson twice before her request and once after. Eventually, at the Last Supper, Jesus demonstrated how important this value was for a Christ-follower when he, the Messiah, tenderly washed the feet of the Twelve, acting as a servant, doing the most menial and dirty task. He would tell them, "I have set you an example that you should do as I have done for you. Very truly I tell you, no servant is greater than his master, nor is a messenger greater than the one who sent him" (John 13:15–16 NIV). But James and John had not yet internalized this lesson. Instead, they confidently proclaimed that they could drink the cup Jesus was about to drink.

Jesus told them they will indeed have to drink from his cup one day. This metaphor of the cup was foretelling the suffering Jesus was about to undergo physically through the crucifixion and spiritually by being forsaken by his Heavenly Father. Little did James and John or Salome know that both men would indeed suffer for the sake of Christ's kingdom.

At some point this misplaced and self-focused ambition turned into a kingdom-focused ambition for James and John. And it probably did for Salome too. Salome saw Jesus killed right before her eyes. And it was Salome—not James or John— who was with the other women at the tomb and went down in history as an eye-witness to Jesus' resurrection. She may have even been with the group of women who saw the resurrected

Jesus in bodily form as they left the tomb, as described in
Matthew's version of events (Matt. 28:1-10). Salome went back
and told her own sons Jesus was alive! Even though we don't
see her again in Scripture, her God encounter was like no other.
Did she now begin to understand what it meant for the first to
be last, and the last to be first? It seemed like her sons finally
understood it, due to their willingness to suffer just like Jesus
said they would. If she lived long enough, no doubt Salome's
heart broke when James became the first of the twelve disciples
to die for his faith (Acts 12:2). And then John was exiled to the
island of Patmos where he wrote the book of Revelation (Rev.
1:9). Just as Salome bore witness to Christ's resurrection, so
did her sons, and in doing so they both drank the cup of Jesus'
suffering in their own ways, just as Jesus prophesied they would.

    And Salome? What about her? Her sons learned what it
meant for the last to be first and the first to be last, and no doubt
she did too. They gave their lives for the gospel, and it was their
greatest ambition to do so. Salome's example shows us how to
have a godly ambition for our children's lives too. So often we
want *less* than God wants for our children. We have good plans
for them: sports, schools, careers, financial comfort. But could
we be holding them back from God's best for their lives by just
settling for what everyone else desires? Perhaps our ambition
is misplaced, like Salome's? Not everyone will or should go into
full-time Christian ministry, missions, or will lay down their
life for the gospel. But all of us who follow Jesus are called to
live for a kingdom that operates in a completely different way
than the world. In this kingdom the first shall be last and the
last shall be first. Being kingdom-focused doesn't mean we

demean ourselves, have no self-esteem, put ourselves down, have false humility, or grovel. It just means we look for ways to serve others by sharing the gospel with them as well as meeting their physical needs if we are able. And Salome's encounter with Jesus shows us how to enter that kingdom.

SALOME'S GOD ENCOUNTER:

Salome, the mother of James and John, asked Jesus to grant her sons special status in his kingdom, which she imagined—like many others—would be fulfilled on earth. This revealed her misplaced ambition of status for her sons. Eventually, Salome learned that the first shall be last and the last shall be first, and her sons lived this out until the end of their lives.

GETTING TO THE HEART

Read Matthew 20:20–28, 27:55–56; Mark 15:40–41, 16:1–8.

Is your ambition kingdom focused? Do you care about unbelievers and want good for them? Do you share the gospel? All around you is a living, breathing mission field; kingdom work can be lived out in the normal everyday life by loving your neighbors and co-workers.

Am I displaying a kingdom-focused ambition for my kids? If they are unbelievers, my first job is to be a witness to them, just as Salome witnessed to her own sons that Jesus was alive.

If my kids are believers, do I lead my kids to love and participate in the local church? Do I encourage them to view the world in a countercultural way where they will be following Jesus by washing the feet of others, so to speak, instead of promoting themselves?

A Prayer for Kingdom Ambition

LORD, I AM SURROUNDED BY THE PRIDE
of self-promotion in social media, the news, and in
the corporate world. Help me not be ashamed to be a
servant like Jesus was when he picked up a towel and
washed his disciple's feet. I pray that the Holy Spirit
would give me eyes to see what you are calling me
to do specifically to bring your kingdom to earth.
We all have different roles and gifts—help me be
effective in mine, and help me pass on this
kingdom mindset to my children.

Eunice and Lois

INSTILLING FAITH IN OUR CHILDREN

Timothy leans closer to the oil lamp, straining his eyes to read Paul's most recent letter. Paul is in Rome and in prison for a second time. The Roman emperor Nero has been intensely persecuting Christians ever since the Great Fire. Terrifying reports have come out of Rome about Christians being arrested and killed in the most dreadful ways, from being fed to wild animals to being lit on fire to illuminate Nero's gardens.[16] Timothy fervently prays such a death does not await Paul, whom he thinks of as a father. He focuses on Paul's opening greeting:

> To Timothy, my dearly loved son.
>
> Grace, mercy, and peace from God the Father and Christ Jesus our Lord.
>
> I thank God, whom I serve with a clear conscience as my ancestors did, when I constantly remember you in my prayers night and day. Remembering your tears, I long to see you so that I may be filled with joy. I recall your sincere faith that first lived in your grandmother Lois and in your mother Eunice and now, I am convinced, is in you also.
>
> Therefore, I remind you to rekindle the gift of God that is in you through the laying on of my hands. For God has not given us a spirit of fear, but one of power, love, and sound judgment. (2 Timothy. 1:2–7 CBS)

The letter continues, reminding Timothy not to be ashamed of the gospel and to continue the work of the church where Timothy is currently ministering in Ephesus. But it also makes it clear that Paul does not expect to escape his imprisonment: "The time for my departure has come. I have fought the good fight, I have finished the race, I have kept the faith" (2 Tim. 4:6–7). Timothy's eyes cloud over in tears at these words. How he hopes the same can be said of him one day!

Towards the end of the letter Paul asks to see Timothy again, before winter if possible.

Timothy rolls up the letter and carefully puts it away with his other correspondence. He will gather the supplies Paul requested in his letter—his cloak, scrolls of papyrus, and parchments—and begin making plans for his journey.

A SINCERE FAITH

Timothy was a young man who had accompanied Paul on his previous missionary journeys and was essentially being mentored by him in the faith. Paul first met Timothy in Lystra, located in the Roman province of Galatia. We are told in Acts 16:1 that Timothy was the son of a woman who was a Jewish believer, but that his father was a Greek (Gentile). His mother's name was Eunice and his grandmother was called Lois. All we really know about them is what Paul says in 2 Timothy 1:5: "I recall your [Timothy's] sincere faith that first lived in your grandmother Lois and in your mother Eunice and now, I am convinced, is in you also" (CSB). The Greek word used for sincere has been translated as "genuine" (NKJV), "unfeigned" (KJV), and also means "without hypocrisy"?[17] We don't have any record whatsoever of Lois or Eunice's God encounter, but we know they had one. They are simply mentioned in passing as having influenced their grandson and son's faith.

But that is not a simple thing. Chances are you and I are more like Lois and Eunice than many of the other women whose stories we've followed. We won't have books written about us to record the story of our lives like Eve or Sarah. We won't be remembered as the mother of a prophet or the Son of God like Hannah or Mary. We are humble people who, when we die, will leave only the legacy of our normal everyday lives behind. We will be remembered for the lives we've touched, and if we have children, they will be our living legacy. We may only have a passing line written about us.

But like Lois and Eunice, we too can have sincere faith. And that faith can change the lives of our children, who will in turn affect the lives of their children, friends, and co-workers. Despite all the "how to be a good Christian parent" books that exist in the world, it's really that simple: our faith will influence our children's faith. We don't need the latest devotional or apologetics course to do that. We just need to have a sincere, unfeigned, unhypocritical faith. Not faith in ourselves or our own ability to be a good parent, but faith in the work of Christ in our hearts to save and change us. Paul goes on to define our faith in the gospel as "the power of God, who saved us and called us to a holy calling, not because of our works but because of his own purpose and grace, which he gave us in Christ Jesus before the ages began, and which now has been manifested through the appearing of our Savior Christ Jesus, who abolished death and brought life and immortality to light through the gospel, for which I was appointed a preacher and apostle and teacher, which is why I suffer as I do" (2 Tim. 1:8-12). What an amazing inheritance to steward!

We won't do it perfectly; we've already seen in the lives of the women whose stories we've followed that they didn't do it perfectly either. They messed up. Sarah doubted God's promises, Leah was jealous, Naomi was bitter, and Bathsheba could have lived in shame her whole life because of what happened to her. The Bible is unfailingly honest and never puts people on pedestals. "No other book narrates with such utter candor the weaknesses of its heroes, and things so contrary to ideals which it aims to promote."[18] But these mothers' encounters with God changed them, slowly, over time. Sometimes God even worked through the legacy of their lives long after they were gone.

Perhaps the most important thing about our faith is that we honestly live what we profess, resisting the temptation to hide our sin and become a hypocrite. Religiosity without sincerity will drive our children away. They will know if we are just putting on a Christian cultural show. It's always okay to admit when we are wrong and ask for their forgiveness if we've realized our faith hasn't been sincere. But it's also a good moment to pause and ask ourselves: *is* my faith a sincere one?

KNOWING SACRED SCRIPTURE

The only other passage that can be construed to possibly refer indirectly to Lois and Eunice is 2 Timothy 3:14-15, which says, in the context of facing persecution—a frighteningly real possibility at that time—"But as for you, continue in what you have learned and firmly believed. You know those who taught you, and you know that from infancy you have known the sacred Scriptures, which are able to give you wisdom for salvation through faith in Christ Jesus" (CSB). Here Paul mentions Timothy having known the Scriptures "from infancy" or, as some other translations say, "childhood."

Here again we have the simplicity of sharing God's word with our children. Fancy Sunday school programs, vacation Bible schools, and curriculums aren't required. Nothing is wrong with those things, and they can be fun. But the consistent exposure to God's word over the entire life of a child can bring life all its own. Actually, right after the passage above in 2 Timothy, Paul pens these famous lines, "All Scripture is breathed out by God and profitable for teaching, for reproof, for correction, and for training in righteousness, that the man of God may be competent, equipped for every good work" (3:16-17). It was Lois and Eunice's sincere faith and the consistent exposure to Scripture that did a work in Timothy's life and enabled him to partner with Paul and lead the church in Ephesus.

What does this look like? It looks like living our lives. It looks like walking with Jesus and sharing that walk with our kids. Deuteronomy gives us a picture of this kind of life when it says:

> Love the LORD your God with all your heart, with all your soul, and with all your strength. These words that I am giving you today are to be in your heart. Repeat them to your children. Talk about them when you sit in your house and when you walk along the road, when you lie down and when you get up. Bind them as a sign on your hand and let them be a symbol on your forehead. Write

them on the doorposts of your house and on your city gates. (6:5-9 CSB)

Again, we see a simple outline for our lives. Love God sincerely first, then share that love with your children. Leave the result to God. We may plant and water, but God is the one who makes faith grow (1 Cor. 3:7). I'm not talking about abdicating our responsibility to teach and protect our children—that is what the planting and watering is for. But we can ultimately rest and trust our children to Jesus' care. Like Jochebed did. Like Hannah did. Like Mary did. It may be scary. If Timothy did indeed go to Rome to visit Paul, and Lois and Eunice were still alive, they would have had to entrust Timothy's safety in Rome to God. Christians were literally being burned alive and he was going to visit Paul, who was already in chains for his faith. By going to Rome, he would put himself in a more dangerous circumstance by associating with Paul. We parents must entrust our children's physical and spiritual safety to the only one who can really protect them.

A CLOUD OF WITNESSES

Sometimes I hear people say that we are living in the worst era in history for Christians to live out their faith. Ironically, the people who've said this to me don't live in a place of severe religious persecution, like many in our world *truly* do. Where I happen to live, it's no worse than times past. It's no worse than when Pharaoh enslaved Israel and ordered the death of all Israel's male children. Or when Moses grew up in an Egyptian household, surrounded by a pagan faith, or when Samuel grew up exposed to a corrupted Israelite faith. Nor is it worse than when Herod ordered the death of all the male children, or when Nero lit the bodies of Christians as torches for his garden. Where I live, it's no worse than it was for first-century Christians, whose children would have seen slaves in the marketplace, pagan temple worship, and crucified bodies hanging in agony along the roads. The women in whose sandals we've walked did not have a pearl-clutching cultural faith that existed in a bubble where they expected everyone to believe the same thing they did. They had *sincere* faith. And we walk in the footsteps they've left for us.

Hebrews says that we are surrounded by a great cloud of witnesses. No doubt some of those witnesses are Jocabed, Naomi, and the Shunammite Woman. No doubt they are Elizabeth, Mary, and Salome. They are cheering us on as we run our race. My husband had a wise grandmother named Caroline Eller, who once encouraged me with these words: "Keep on track and run the good race. Do not look to the people in the stands who are cheering or booing you. Do not go into the stands to defend yourself. Look only to God."

We are to fix our eyes on Jesus. That is all. Only him. Each of these mothers has shown us how God used their motherhood to encounter him, and their lives were never the same. He's the goal. He's the prize. He will run alongside us in every trial, will carry us when we are weary, and he will take us home.

LOIS AND EUNICE'S GOD ENCOUNTER:

Though only mentioned briefly, these two women were praised for their influence on Timothy, who would become vital to the Apostle Paul's ministry. How do they do it? By having a sincere faith and consistently exposing their son and grandson to Scripture throughout his childhood.

GETTING TO THE HEART

Read Acts 16:1–5; 2 Timothy 1:2–5; 2 Timothy 3:14–15.

Is your faith sincere? Have you accepted Jesus' invitation to be Lord of your life?

Do you share Scripture with your kids on a regular basis regardless of their age? Besides reading the Bible we can also memorize verses together, write notes to our kids with Scriptural encouragement, and remind them of what the Bible says in daily conversation.

How will your sincere faith affect and influence the next generation? This applies to all of us whether we have biological children or not. Are there others who come to mind whose lives God is nudging you to speak into or encourage?

A Prayer for Sincere Faith

LORD, I PRAY FOR SINCERE FAITH.
Help me not accept a cultural faith that is
passed down due to hypocritical religiosity.
May I not go to church and then look down on the
"sinners" like the Pharisees did. True righteousness
is not shocked by the sinner but reaches out to love
them where they are. You called us into the world, so let
my faith be real, alive, and sincere so that it shines like
a light in the dark places. But it will only shine if I'm
actually in the world, not a religious bubble.
Help me be willing to entrust my kids as they go out
into the sometimes dangerous world. May the sincerity
of my faith influence the next generation: my kids,
my kids' friends, my friends' kids. Help my faith
give birth to faith in the next generation.

NOTES

1. Leigh McLeroy, *Treasured: Knowing God by the Things He Keeps* (Colorado Springs: WaterBrook Press, 2009), 44.

2. E. Randolph Richards and Richard James, *Misreading Scripture with Individualistic Eyes: Patronage, Honor, and Shame in the Biblical World* (Downers Grove, IL: IVP Academic, 2020), 52.

3. "The Powerful Solanaceae: Mandrake," US Forest Service, accessed August 13, 2024, https://www.fs.usda.gov/wildflowers/ethnobotany/Mind_and_Spirit/mandrake.shtml.

4. Henry H. Halley, *Halley's Bible Handbook: An Abbreviated Bible Commentary*, 24th ed. (Grand Rapids, MI: Zondervan, 1965), 104.

5. Halley, *Halley's Bible Handbook*, 177.

6. Gien Karssen, *Her Name is Woman: 24 Women of the Bible* (Colorado Springs, CO: NavPress, 1975), 86.

7. James Strong, *Strong's Exhaustive Concordance of the Bible* (Peabody, MA: Hendrickson Publishers, 2007), 1535.

8. *Ruth and Samuel* (Colorado Springs, CO: Community Bible Study, 2023), 181.

9. Strong, *Strong's Exhaustive Concordance of the Bible*, 1582.

10. Tara-Leigh Cobble, *The Bible Recap: A One-Year Guide to Reading and Understanding the Entire Bible* (Minneapolis, MN: Bethany House, 2020), 282.

11. Fredrick Dale Bruner, *The Christbook: A Historical/Theological Commentary* (Waco: Word Books, 1987), vol. 1, p. 6, quoted in Bob Deffinbaugh, "The Origins of Jesus Christ," Bible.org, accessed August 13, 2024, https://bible.org/seriespage/1-origins-jesus-christ-matthew-11-25#P54_17322.

12. T.S. Eliot, *The Complete Poems and Plays 1909–1950* (New York: Harcourt Brace & Company, 1980), 145.

13. Elisabeth Elliot, *Secure in the Everlasting Arms: Trusting the God Who Never Leaves Your Side* (Ann Arbor, MI: Vine Books, 2002), 176–177.

14. C.S. Lewis, *Yours, Jack: Spiritual Direction with C.S. Lewis*, ed. Paul F. Ford (New York: Harper One, 2008), 97–98.

15. Karssen, *Her Name is Woman*, 139.

16. Halley, *Halley's Bible Handbook*, 635.

17. Strong, *Strong's Exhaustive Concordance of the Bible*, 1606.

18. Halley, *Halley's Bible Handbook*, 104.

ACKNOWLEDGMENTS

Fourteen years ago, I started this book as a series of blog posts while pregnant with my third child. I couldn't find a book that told biblical mothers' stories in a narrative style, so I decided to start writing one. It's been quite a journey to seeing these words on the printed page, and my prayer as I've written it has come from 2 Corinthians 9:8: "And God is able to make every grace overflow to you, so that in every way, always having everything you need, you may excel in every good work" (CSB). I prayed God would give me everything I needed to write this book—most importantly his words—so that this work would be "good."

Thank you to the Square Halo team for believing in this message and making it possible for the words to reach its readers.

Josh, thank you for loving me, encouraging me, and reading this book from beginning to end with helpful suggestions, edits, and corrections.

Duncan, Owen, Sophia, and Ava, you gave me space to write this book. You helped me get it done.

Mom, you've modeled what it means to be a praying mother so well. Thanks for your prayers while writing.

Jennifer Kinard, Alison Kersten, and Amy Kannel, thank you for reading various portions of this book and giving feedback, corrections, and suggestions. Invaluable!

Jill Lewis, thank you for watching my kids and taking them to the pool so I could write and they could have fun over the summer.

Mostly, I'm thankful to God, who used the stories of these fifteen women to encourage, challenge, and strengthen my own faith, even as I share their stories with you.

About the Author

DANIELLE AYERS JONES has always loved to tell stories: whether with paper and pen or behind the lens, it's one of the things she loves to do best. That passion led her to receive a double major in English and Graphic Design from York College of Pennsylvania. In past careers she told stories by working as an exhibition designer for The Walters Art Museum and as a family photographer. Her writing has been featured in publications like *Common Place Quarterly, iBelieve, The Joyful Life Magazine,* and on her website danielleayersjones.com.

Danielle lives in Maryland with her husband, four children, and a dog named Ember. Her days are filled with homeschooling and lots of coffee. She likes to relax with a thick novel or a nature hike.

more from Square Halo Books

WILD THINGS AND CASTLES IN THE SKY: A GUIDE TO CHOOSING THE BEST BOOKS FOR CHILDREN

"An inspiring and immensely practical gift from forty wise and well-read people to those who want to bring up children marked by meaning."—Anselm Society

GODLY CHARACTER(S): INSIGHTS FOR SPIRITUAL PASSION FROM THE LIVES OF 8 WOMEN IN THE BIBLE

By conforming our character to God's design, we can awaken in our hearts a sincere love for him, driving us into deeper intimacy with God and leading us to greater joy in our daily lives.

SPEAKING CODE: UNRAVELING PAST BONDS TO REDEEM BROKEN CONVERSATIONS

We long for soul satisfying conversations characterized by truth spoken in love, but everyone is *speaking code.* This book helps us decipher cryptic conversations, allowing us to see where God's goodness enters our lives.

TINY THOUGHTS THAT I'VE BEEN THINKING: SELECTED WRITINGS OF LESLIE ANNE BUSTARD

A magpie's nest of reflections on art, faith, literature, community, caregiving, and mortality, these essays, poems, and miscellaneous musings demonstrate how one follower of Jesus lived life to the glory of God by adding to the Beauty in the world around her.

SQUAREHALOBOOKS.com